The 4 ESSENTIALS

of Entrepreneurial Thinking

What Successful People Didn't Learn in School

CLIFF MICHAELS

Praise

*"Cliff Michaels delivers a powerful path to
profits, passion, and purpose."*
TONY HSIEH
CEO, Zappos.com, #1 NY Times Bestselling Author - *Delivering Happiness*

*"Cliff's writing is full of creativity, inspiration, and practical lessons.
Whether you're a student or professional, I highly recommend this book."*
BLAKE MYCOSKIE
Founder, Chief Shoe Giver, TOMS Shoes
#1 NY Times Bestselling Author - *Start Something That Matters*

*"The 4 Essentials is a fun read.
Like Cliff, it's full of passion with a blend of new ideas and timeless wisdom."*
DAVE LOGAN
Former Associate Dean, USC Marshall Business School
#1 NY Times Bestselling Co-Author - *Tribal Leadership*

*"A visionary leader and pioneering entrepreneur, Cliff Michaels sets the
bar for life and business training. The 4 Essentials is a winning formula."*
MICHAEL CAITO
International Chairman, Entrepreneurs' Organization

*"Intelligent and highly recommended!
Cliff has that rare ability to connect with people at all levels."*
ALLANA BARONI
Featured Contributor for Socializing on Oprah.com, Author - *Get Social*

*"Cliff's concept for a Master's in Basic Abilities
hits the nail on the head. He takes us on a life journey with pragmatic
insights, offering a guide for anyone on their entrepreneurial path."*
SUE HESSE
Director, Foundation Partnerships, The Kauffman Foundation

The 4 Essentials of Entrepreneurial Thinking
What Successful People Didn't Learn in School

© Copyright 2011 By Cliff Michaels

First Edition
Published by Cliff Michaels & Associates, Inc.

www.cliffmichaels.com
www.the4essentials.com

ISBN 13 #: 978-0-615-45055-1

Dedication

To my nieces and nephews » Jenny, Rachel, Ian, Ryan, Ethan

Much love

To the misfits, dreamers, and risk-takers

Carpe diem

Mission

*Inspire, give back, and raise the bar
for education and entrepreneurship.*

Giving Back

*With each book you purchase,
a FREE book is donated to a student.
10% proceeds also go to charities.*

Share the Buzz

CliffMichaels.com

Acknowledgements

*"In my walks, every man I meet
is my superior in some way, and in that, I learn from him."*
RALPH WALDO EMERSON (1803 – 1882)
American Poet, Philosopher

A MILLION THANKS ...

To my sisters, Gigi and Eve » Thanks for unconditional love and the midnight nosh. You always gave me a place to talk and laugh it out.

To esteemed colleagues spreading great ideas at TEDTalks, Young Presidents' Organization (YPO), Entrepreneurs' Organization (EO), and The Aspen Institute » Continue raising the bar for education and entrepreneurship.

To countless mentors responsible for my real-world education through the years » This book is my mission to pay it forward.

To interns, students, and **campus organizations** for tireless contribution to my work » Your imagination has no boundaries. Keep rockin' the boat!

To selfless volunteers who teach us about giving and gratitude » Namaste.

To special friends » Your support was instrumental to this book » Allana Baroni, Michael Caito, Sally DeLuca, Scott Duffy, Judy & Tony East, Amir Esfahani, Mohammed Fathelbab, Kasra Ferasat, Nicole Frank, Brandon Franzke, Neema & David Ghannadi, Ridgely Goldsborough, Dan Goldstone, Rich Halvorson, Milad Hassani, Christine Hassler, Troy Hazard, Patrick Henry, Sue Hesse, Craig Honick, Shep Hyken, Mary Leonida, Gene Lim, Ross Loehner, Dave Logan, Adrian Mason, Mary Mazzio, Doug Mellinger, Bill Milliken, Kam Najmi, Nina Nazar, Jason Niedle, Chris Novy, Steve Phillips, Marsha Ralls, Rob Richman, Jason & Jayme Riggio, Sam Roham, Michael Shillan, Diane Sillan, Jake Strom, Jim Weldon.

To **my parents** » Thanks for the gift of an adventurous soul.

To Inspirational Mentors

Thanks for sharing your passion and vision.

Artists, Leaders, Writers
Scientists, Teachers, Philosophers

Maya Angelou, Aristotle, The Beatles, Warren Bennis, Jeff Bezos, Richard Branson, Buddha, Warren Buffett, Dale Carnegie, Charlie Chaplin, Confucius, Stephen Covey, Charles Darwin, Leonardo da Vinci, Ellen DeGeneres, Charles Dickens, Walt Disney, Peter Drucker, Thomas Edison, Albert Einstein, Ralph Waldo Emerson, Aretha Franklin, Benjamin Franklin, Galileo Galilei, Mohandas Gandhi, Howard Gardner, Bill and Melinda Gates, Kahlil Gibran, Malcolm Gladwell, Seth Godin, Jane Goodall, Daniel Goleman, Stephen Hawking, Napoleon Hill, Tony Hsieh, Helen Keller, Elisabeth Kubler-Ross, Steve Jobs, Bruce Lee, Abraham Lincoln, Martin Luther King, Jr., Nelson Mandela, A.A. Milne, Margaret Mead, Wolfgang Mozart, Blake Mycoskie, Pablo Picasso, Friedrich Nietzsche, Tony Robbins, Charlie Rose, J.K. Rowling, Howard Schultz, William Shakespeare, Will Smith, Socrates, Steven Spielberg, Oliver Stone, Henry David Thoreau, J.R.R. Tolkien, Mark Twain, Sun Tzu, Oscar Wilde, Oprah Winfrey, Stevie Wonder, 14th Dalai Lama.

Comedians, Satirists, Cartoonists

Woody Allen, Lucille Ball, Mel Brooks, Carol Burnett, George Carlin, Stephen Colbert, Bill Cosby, Billy Crystal, Ellen DeGeneres, Tina Fey, Matt Groening, Steve Martin, The Marx Brothers, Mike Myers, Richard Pryor, Chris Rock, Charles M. Schulz, Jerry Seinfeld, Jon Stewart, Robin Williams, Steven Wright.

Sports Legends

Muhammad Ali, Lance Armstrong, Wayne Gretzky, Mia Hamm, Tony Hawk, Magic Johnson, Pelé, Jackie Robinson, Vin Scully, John Wooden, Tiger Woods.

Table of Contents

Genesis of The 4 Essentials

"Why don't schools teach this stuff?"

F OR THE RECORD, I don't have a degree. I'm not a university professor nor do I play one on TV. At best, I'm a part-time philosopher and full-time truth-seeker. Growing up, I never felt like I fit in. Not at home. Not at school. Certainly not the future I was staring at in my late teens. Then I had a life-changing moment. I was just a year out of high school at the University of Southern California when a friendly dialogue with students and professors reached a fever pitch. As I listened to a debate about prerequisite courses, rising tuition fees, and the value of a degree, I decided to chime in. I was just an undergraduate trying to find my way, and maybe, just maybe, rock the boat a little.

At the time, I was learning the real estate game from street-wise mentors and picking up a few basic life skills. I had never even heard the word *entrepreneur* until I was 18, but the whole idea of gaps in the education system fascinated me. I soon found myself conducting an extra-credit survey to prove a simple theory ...

REAL-WORLD ESSENTIALS
CRITICAL TO SUCCESS

I wasn't the first and I won't be the last to have this epiphany, but why didn't schools teach the stuff I was learning as a young entrepreneur — networking, negotiations, team building, creative thinking, problem solving, and time management? Short of elite business schools, was anyone connecting real-world success principles?

I soon polled honor students, esteemed professors, and a range of highly successful professionals. I looked for common threads. Years later, I researched everyone from Socrates, Edison, and da Vinci, to modern-day icons like Jobs, Gates, Oprah, and Branson. I even studied top athletes and musicians — what could they teach us about peak performance? Who defines success anyway, and the best way to get there — the artist, billionaire, humanitarian? Ambitious but broke, I left college early and began a knowledge quest. This book is the 20-year result of that journey; a missing link between what traditional education teaches and *The 4 Essentials* critical to real-world success.

If I Knew Then What I Know Now

I wrote this book wishing I had been taught so much more at an earlier age. I also hope this book addresses the 800-pound gorilla in academic, corporate, and political circles; that traditional education still needs a 21st century overhaul. This doesn't mean college degrees and corporate-training programs aren't valuable. They certainly are. Let's just say there's a strong case *4 Essentials* are of equal value.

In the following pages, you'll read about books, movies, childhood idols, and modern to historical figures that had a profound impact on my life. Each chapter was based on real-world lessons that shaped my journey as a young entrepreneur. I learned from so many mentors and experiences that no single lesson could ever be described as *the secret*. Nonetheless, there were watershed moments. I promise to share them all.

With gratitude,

Cliff Michaels

Introduction

"We are what we repeatedly do.
Excellence, then, is not an act, but a habit."
ARISTOTLE (384 BC – 322 BC)
Greek Philosopher

A Peak Performance Playbook

EVER WONDER WHY CERTAIN individuals seem smarter, happier, or exceptional in their field? Is it luck? Are they born with innate abilities and superior genes? How about supportive parents, special mentors, or dynamic communities? Well, let's not kid ourselves — these advantages can be a serious leg up in life or business.

No doubt, higher education, great teachers, and the best schools are also important. Statistically, those who learn more, earn more. However, not even an advanced degree is a proxy for success (or happiness). How do we explain the countless stories of smart, well-educated, or privileged people who struggle repeatedly in life? On the flipside, we marvel at highly successful people who never graduated from college such as Richard Branson, Lucille Ball, Thomas Edison, Bill Gates, or The Beatles. The dropout list is a veritable Who's Who of misfits, millionaires, billionaires, scientific pioneers, champion athletes, artistic geniuses, and creative entrepreneurs. Others transcend culture clashes and language barriers in spite of poverty or learning challenges.

Conclusion? The very notion that an individual's success is predicated solely on talent, intelligence, financial advantage, or traditional education is categorically false. There's a peak-performance playbook that has nothing to do with opportunity or gifts at birth. Best of all, the playbook has an agnostic set of principles anyone can learn, regardless of age or background. In fact, the playbook assumes most of us are not born with great talent, superior intelligence, or economic privilege. So what do extraordinary people have in common?

It's quite simple ...

Successful people connect *4 Essentials of Entrepreneurial Thinking.*

1 Basic Life Skills

2 Action Strategies

3 Core Values

4 Purpose Principles

Bridging the Gaps

Consider the talents of great men and women through time. From Greek philosophers to modern moguls, did anyone really achieve success at birth? Not even close; including the so-called genius or born entrepreneur.

FACT: We all have gaps.

Sure, many are fortunate to have those great genes, supportive parents, or an environment to foster talent. History tells us however that none of these gifts by themselves produce results. Moreover, if we measure success not merely by wealth and accolades, but health, happiness, and contribution, we know true abundance requires a much larger set of *Essentials* than any of us are born with. This leads to a fundamental question. If there's a simple formula for highly-connected success principles, why wouldn't we teach it in every classroom or training program and in every field of study?

Can't everyone benefit from a real-world MBA?

a **Master's** in **Basic Abilities**

A Paradigm Shift in Global Education

If the purpose of a degree or specialized training is to achieve life and career excellence, standards for teaching success principles must be higher than ever. Today's generation has enough pressure knowing it's the first since World War II on a track to do worse than it's parents.

Fortunately, many schools and success trainers are catching on. They're teaching principles in this book. I didn't invent them. However, *The 4 Essentials* are rarely taught in concert with one another. At best, the connection is fragmented. At worst, basic education is void of personal growth and entrepreneurial thinking, even in the best high schools or top universities.

At the core are even bigger challenges. Rising costs and entry requirements for higher education can be extreme. As a result, young professionals often fall into dysfunctional peer groups and workplaces. They stop learning at an early age or build poor habits. In turn, not everyone brings critical abilities to competitive environments. This is a recipe for limited growth and high failure rates.

Is there a solution? Yes! However, the idea that success training begins or ends in a classroom remains flawed. The quality of education is the direct result of how we teach, share, and practice success principles for life. Peer-to-peer learning is just as relevant as instructor-to-classroom. This is as true for artists as it is for executives. To that end, *The 4 Essentials* provide a basic system to maximize strengths and minimize weaknesses; to leverage entrepreneurial thinking.

Once the foundation is laid, a high school student can incorporate skills and strategies of a college graduate. A business leader can develop the high-performance routines of a world-class athlete. An activist can adopt the purpose principles of mentors who changed the world.

In *The 4 Essentials*, we also discover that the sooner these principles are practiced, the sooner we accelerate peak performance in all areas of our personal and professional lives. It's simply a matter of connecting the dots:

Skills · Strategies · Values · Purpose

How This Book is Structured

1 This book is divided into 5 parts. I'll start with *My Lessons from the Edge* to give you a better idea of who I am and how this book started.

2 After my journey, we'll jump into *The 4 Essentials*. I wrote these lessons over many years, mostly to share whimsical quotes, fun essays, and success principles with clients and friends. Initially, there was no framework. In this book however, many topics dovetail from one to the next. I suggest reading chapters in order, at least the first time.

3 Some lessons are short and bloggy. Others have a story angle. Either way, please don't call the publishing police. A little informality will make our conversation more interesting.

4 **Exercises + Story Contest** » If you're up for a challenge, this book includes a contest at the end of *Essential* chapters. RULES + ENTRY FORMS AT www.cliffmichaels.com.

Ready?

Let's have some fun!

Chapter 1
Early Childhood

*"I was too naïve to know what I couldn't do,
so most of the time I just did it."*
Reflection

Midnight — Summer, Santa Monica, 2011

It's been twenty years since I conceived this book. Final draft is in sight. Friends say my favorite Oscar Wilde quote should go right here:

"Be yourself — everyone else is taken."

Okay, Here Goes Nothing:

- I'm a semi-dyslexic insomniac.
- I wasn't a born entrepreneur; just a misfit.
- Sometimes I talk too much — I could listen more.
- I might be attention deficit. Did you see that squirrel moonwalk?
- My best-kept secret? I don't own a suit. A jacket over jeans has to pass for reluctantly fashionable. All things being equal, I'd rather be naked.

Somehow, with all my foibles, I found success and never regretted failures along the way. That said, if 30-something Cliff could chat with 20-something Cliff, *ohhh* the conversations we'd have ...

Tales of a Soccer Kid

I WAS BORN IN New York City, 1967, the baby brother of two sisters, Gigi and Eve. I was a short, scrawny kid with a gift for gab. Gift for gab is kid-speak for occasionally witty and hard to shut up.

My parents are Jewish, originally from Brooklyn. Mom and Dad divorced as early as I can remember and rarely spoke again. Mom is a retired nurse who enjoys live theater. Dad is a psychiatrist and neurologist who fancies himself a renaissance man, but with a Groucho Marx complex. I didn't live with my dad but we enjoyed tons of Dodger baseball games. Those hours at the ballpark gave us a common vocabulary for sports, books, and dirty jokes.

We moved to Tenafly, New Jersey when I was a baby, then Southern California when I was 5. We moved eight more times before I was 12, mostly downsizing middle-class neighborhoods from Encino to Woodland Hills in the San Fernando Valley. My childhood was neither privileged nor underprivileged, but home life was a bit dysfunctional. As the youngest, I was oblivious to family squabbles and tuned out most of the noise. My sisters and I lived with my mom but we were years apart and didn't hang out much. Like many siblings, we became closer as adults and always shared a special bond.

Both parents were too busy to watch over us kids, so we had no family structure. To the contrary, Gigi, Eve, and I were left to our own devices. The girls moved out early, Gigi at 15 and Eve at 17. I love my sisters madly. They always checked in on little Cliffy and for that, I'm eternally grateful. As for me, most of the time anyway, I was a home-alone kid, starved for attention.

In spite of a disjointed upbringing and nine different schools from kindergarten to high school, I was a good student. On occasion, I played hooky to hang out at beaches, libraries, and local arcades. That was the extent of my shenanigans. Wild kid, huh? With no parental supervision, it's amazing I didn't get into trouble, but I was fortunate to be a bookworm (a gift from both parents I suppose). I often escaped to my favorite novelists; among them Twain, Dickens, and Salinger. These early mentors taught me about humor and hope, good versus evil, and the inequities of life. They also inspired me to write.

It's fair to say I'm a movie buff, music maven, and comedy nut. My earliest influences were Steven Spielberg, The Beatles, and George Carlin. I'm also nostalgic for classic cartoons like Bugs Bunny, Charlie Brown, and Winnie the Pooh. If you're too cool for cartoons, you're too cool for me.

At the heart of my DNA, I was a sports junkie. I played everything from tennis to baseball, but soccer was my year-round passion. At 9, I was selected to play for a club team called the Junior Aztecs. We were sponsored by the Los

Angeles Aztecs, a professional club of the former North American Soccer League. We even got to train a bit with the pros and play a few games at the Rose Bowl in front of live crowds — quite a trip for a soccer kid.

At the time, Brazilian soccer legend, Pelé, came out of retirement to play for the New York Cosmos, a cross-country rival of the Aztecs. My first memory of Pelé was watching him fly through the air, scoring on a bicycle kick. Dreams of a professional career soon danced in my head. For those who don't know his story, Pelé was so poor his neighborhood team was known as *The Shoeless Ones*. At 16 however, he was selected to Brazil's national team. At 17, he scored six goals in the 1958 World Cup, skyrocketing to international fame. He would ultimately lead Brazil to three World Cup Championships from 1958 to 1970 and the Cosmos to a championship in 1977. By career's end, Pelé was the indisputable *King of Soccer* with a mind-boggling 1,281 goals in 1,363 games.

The Love Speech

In 1977, Pelé played his farewell game at Giants Stadium, New York; one half for the Cosmos, the other for Santos, his native club from Brazil. I was 10 years old. Before the game, in front of 75,000 screaming fans and a TV audience in 38 countries, Pelé delivered a short speech I would never forget:

> *"I want to take this opportunity to ask you, in this moment when*
> *the world looks to me ... to take more attention to kids all over*
> *the world ... I want to ask you ... because I believe love is*
> *more important than anything we can take from life ...*
> *because everything else passes ... to say with me three times, LOVE."*

With each cry of "LOVE" from Pelé, a jubilant crowd echoed, "LOVE." After the game, 3-Time World Heavyweight Champ, Muhammad Ali, embraced Pelé and said, "There are now two of *The Greatest*." I was too young to appreciate the moment but considering I had no formal mentors growing up, Pelé was a pretty good choice. It's been said he's done more goodwill with his message of "LOVE" than most world leaders. Deservedly, *TIME Magazine* included Pelé on their list of "100 Most Important People of the 20th Century."

Months after his farewell game, I was seeking an autograph from Pelé. Among a swarm of kids at a soccer clinic, I shouted, "What does it take to be a champion?" Pelé flashed his famous smile and said three words, "Practice. Teamwork. Love."

My Soccer Journey

By the time I was 11, our Junior Aztecs had won league titles and played matches in far-off lands from England to Israel. I had a knack for scoring goals and was a fairly good playmaker. At 12, I transferred to a new club, West Valley United. We were the first American team to win one of the largest youth tournaments in the world (The 1981 Robbie), played annually in Canada. I scored two goals in the championship final, the game-winner on a diving header. I was 14 and my confidence couldn't be higher.

Unfortunately, by the time high school rolled around, ankle twists and physical therapy were routine. I played out my senior year but knew I had lost my edge. By 17, ligaments in both ankles were shredded. Although college scouts showed interest, athletic scholarships went down the drain.

By 18, the physical damage was irreparable. Any hopes of a soccer career were crushed. Maybe I was never good enough anyway? I spent half my senior year on crutches, the other half wondering what I would do with the rest of my life. I was emotionally lost.

Fortunately, Pelé's words never escaped my soul. "Practice. Teamwork. Love ..."

Chapter 2
Games, Chess, and Secrets to Success

> *"If ignorant both of your enemy and yourself, you are certain to be in peril ... Know your enemy and know yourself ... and you can fight a hundred battles without disaster."*
> SUN TZU (EST. 6TH CENTURY BC)
> Chinese Military Strategist - *The Art of War*

Life 101

I LEFT HOME A few months before high school ended. I was a double threat, clueless and penniless. I couldn't afford my own place so I crashed on the couch of whatever friend would have me. The idea of college weighed heavy on my mind but my father offered to help with a few semesters of tuition. I still had to navigate the world on my own (food, rent). There's a Life 101 manual, right?

I soon immersed in entrepreneur magazines and self-help books, assuming answers were a page away. Unfortunately, books were usually too dry or full of hype. There were inspirational stories but nothing tangible. Business books were worse. Unless you were a math wiz or card-carrying member of Wall Street, the complex graphs and acronyms were enough to depress anyone, even an ambitious kid like me.

Then one night, I picked up a bit of life wisdom watching a favorite movie ...

"How About a Nice Game of Chess?"

In 1983, Matthew Broderick played a computer wiz-kid named David Lightman in the blockbuster film, *War Games*. In the story, Lightman begins what he thinks is a harmless video game. He soon discovers he's inadvertently hacked into a military computer and nearly triggered the United States into launching a nuclear attack against Russia. The computer is an artificial intelligence system designed to simulate war games — code name: WOPR; short for War Operation Plan Response. WOPR's programming included chess, poker, and tic-tac-toe. In theory, the practice of these strategic games would enable military commanders to learn from mistakes in wartime.

The countdown has begun. Lightman must now save the planet from World War III. Fast-forward to the movie's final scene. War generals and computer gurus at the NORAD Command Center are attempting to stop WOPR from launching a first strike. Just minutes from an apocalypse, Lightman programs the computer to accelerate the learning curve by playing tic-tac-toe against itself. Exhausted from playing futile war games and a tireless loop of tic-tac-toe that always ends in a draw, the computer blows a fuse and shuts down. In the darkness of a quiet war room, a simulated voice addresses the computer's designer. *"Greetings Professor Falken – a strange game – the only winning move is not to play. How about a nice game of chess?"*

Suspending disbelief as a movie critic, what I took away from *War Games* was the idea of a system that teaches us to learn from mistakes. Wouldn't it be cool if we all had a real-world war plan to fight life's battles?

I decided to hit the library and check out a few books on chess. I was fascinated by *War Games* since I played chess but was never very good. My basic curiosity was how many moves a great player can see ahead. What I learned is that Grandmasters, the highest rank a chess player can attain, are never pigeonholed a few moves ahead. They visualize entire game scenarios, adjusting on the fly to a bank of tactics they've practiced for years. They also rely on their knowledge of an adversary as much as textbook strategy. In other words, Grandmasters are as nimble as they are forward-thinking.

A few books later, I connected chess to life skills and brain development. Here's where research got interesting. To become an exceptional chess player, you have to learn six pieces, each with unique shapes, sizes, and abilities. There are literally billions of potential scenarios after an opening move. Risk assessment is constant. Such complexities make chess one of the best games to develop memory and reasoning skills. In turn, these enhanced brain functions make us better in math, reading, and spatial learning. We even develop patience and social intelligence by reading an opponent's body language or facial expressions. Listen up poker players and would-be negotiators — games of chance like Monopoly or one-dimensional video games can't compete for life-skill development.

When I looked back at my childhood, I realized how lucky I was to have developed a few real-world battle skills. Reading provided vocabulary and knowledge; writing instilled creativity and imagination; chess improved memory, logic, and problem solving; soccer provided teamwork, coordination, and disciplined practice — perhaps these *Essentials* would serve me well as an adult?

Back in 1985 however, I had little perspective beyond the classroom or soccer field. Like most teenagers, I was insecure and life was a mystery. How would I earn a living, make time for a girlfriend, or even balance a checkbook? I had moved so many times as a kid that loyal friends were hard to come by. The few friends I had were moving away to different colleges. There were no e-mails or cell phones; no online social networks to make communication easy. I was 18 with no guidance. In my mind, I was alone.

War games? The real world? I knew nothing. I was in survival mode ...

Chapter 3
My Summer Real Estate Camp

*"On the mountains of truth you can never climb in vain ...
either you will reach a point higher up today, or you will be
training your powers ... to climb higher tomorrow."*
FRIEDRICH NIETZSCHE (1844 – 1900)
German Philosopher

Street Practice

ONCE HIGH SCHOOL WAS over, I detailed cars for a little cash but what I really needed was a future game plan. After reading all those business books, I considered real estate. At the time, no-money-down investments were all the rage. Unfortunately, books didn't provide experience and those late-night evangelists with money-maker infomercials struck me as charlatans. So with no such thing as a real-estate boot camp, I hit the housing jungle of Encino, California, my pockets full of nothing but curiosity.

For weeks, I strolled into open houses and real estate offices, asking brokers and homeowners how to buy properties. In time, I met experienced investors who let me tag along. After driving them nuts with endless questions, a few guys shut me up and put me to work as a gopher. My tasks consisted of cold-calls, paperwork, property search, and the proud title of "lunch boy" — fetch Cliff, fetch. Whatever they needed, I listened and learned. Working for pocket money ($100/week), I got one hell of an education. It was nothing like the spare-time riches promised in cheesy seminars. The real world was a boatload of work.

A typical workday began at 7:00 a.m. The guys I worked with specialized in auctions and foreclosures. My job was to follow leads and scope classified ads for new bargains, then make calls to owners, agents, and banks. I did this every morning for hours on end. Then I organized a road map of all the properties. After a quick lunch, I was out knocking on doors and analyzing homes. It was a

9

great way to learn property prices and design.

I usually worked into the night, seven days a week. I must have seen a thousand homes that Summer. By Fall, I had knowledge of loans, contracts, negotiations, and cash-flow analysis. I studied dozens of neighborhoods and kept a property journal. When it came time to make offers, I could recite numbers cold (amenities, square footage, sale comparisons). My hard work also made an impression on the investors I hung out with. I soon realized the big dogs needed little bloodhounds like me. Money they had. Time and energy to sniff out all the deals they didn't.

Since the investors wanted full-time help, I couldn't work for them if I enrolled in college. That was a bummer since I wanted to attend USC. On the flipside, my Summer networking paid an unexpected dividend. By now I had lined up a few partners willing to invest with me if I ever found a bargain property below market — a 25% discount sale was their magic number.

Now I was on a mission! I started building work teams. To get information on properties without running around all day, I made friends with top real-tors, loan officers, and salespeople at title companies. These were the folks who had access to public information that average Joe didn't. When I mentioned "my investors," I soon discovered a world of private offerings and bank-owned bargains (affectionately known as *pocket listings*). Fascinating! Each real estate professional had a vested interest in sharing information because most are paid on commission only. Suddenly deals were chasing me!

Once I built a small network, my follow-up routine consisted of an old-school Rolodex and my trusty notepad, (very high-tech stuff). But of all the lessons I learned that summer, handwritten thank-you notes were the #1 secret to building relationships. I would even leave notes with little, chocolate kisses at a broker's office or homeowner's door step. I became known as the Hershey-Kisses Kid (tuck that nugget away for later).

At Summer's end, I checked back with my dad to see if he would still pay for a year of tuition. He agreed. It was my responsibility to cover all other expenses. So I called a high-school pal and we split rent. We lucked into a cheap, two-bedroom apartment just before the Fall semester. If I could just find that elusive bargain property, I was certain all would be well in my world.

Okay college, here I come ...

Chapter 4
A Unique College Experience

*"We learn by example and by direct experience because
there are real limits to the adequacy of verbal instruction."*
MALCOLM GLADWELL (1963 –)
Canadian Author

In Search of Entrepreneurship

IN THE FALL OF 1985, I enrolled at the University of Southern California. I was the lost freshman with a *Wall Street Journal* under one arm and an entrepreneur book under the other. I didn't understand economics but the idea of business school seemed cool. If nothing else, I wanted to look like I belonged in this strange new world. In reality, I felt out of place. I was social but never joined a fraternity. I didn't drink or party. My angst about money left me with just enough bandwidth to work and study. Sure, I was getting real-world lessons on the street, but I was missing all the fun of a college experience.

Whatever free time I had was used to earn a buck and stretch my entrepreneurial legs: house hunting, house painting, washing cars, and midnight tutoring. Hard working guy? You bet. Smart? Highly debatable. I worked exhausting hours and focus never entered my mind. I had a girlfriend when college started, but the relationship fizzled — I didn't have a clue about managing work and school, let alone romance.

By the end of my freshman year, I was at a financial and emotional crossroads. My lease was up, spirit down, and I had paint on half my clothes. I spent the summer searching properties but I couldn't keep up the pace much longer. If I didn't find a cheaper place to live, I'd need to quit college.

Then one day ...

The Call

A month before my sophomore year, I received a call from Kate, a homeowner I had met one year prior. I stayed in touch with holiday letters, hoping the price would drop on a condo she was selling. Kate was now facing bank foreclosure. The property was an old, vacant rental she hated to manage. When she was ready to dump it cheap, the first call she made was to the one guy who sent a birthday card a few weeks prior — yours truly.

"Cliff, the condo just needs some love — we've neglected it for years, but the deal is yours if you can move fast." said Kate. "I just need someone to buy it before my credit is ruined. You'd be doing me a favor — the bank needs a call Monday!

Wow! She felt I was doing her a favor? Maybe there's something to be said for thank-you notes after all. Within 72 hours, one of my investors stepped up. His name was Bill. I set up negotiations and Bill helped strike a deal with Kate's bank for $90,000 (gotta love the '80s). Kate was thrilled — credit saved! The price was 40% below market so this was a no-brainer for Bill and me. Bill co-signed for a loan and provided the small down payment (less than $5,000). For my part, I would live in the property, fix it up (paint and carpet), cover expenses (rent to roomies), and give up 25% of future profits to Bill. This was a sweet deal for Bill so he was more than fair about how we'd split profits in my favor if I held up my end of the bargain.

In a month's time, I was living in beautiful Hollywood Hills. The condo had two-bedrooms, a pool, and tennis courts. I rented out one room to a few classmates and lived payment-free in the other. That's how I survived year two at USC and started in real estate. Not bad for a sleep-deprived freshman.

Back at USC, friends wanted to know how I pulled off a real estate deal on a student budget. Most of us were scrambling for lunch money so when my roommates told tales of Cliff's Hollywood Hills bachelor pad, I was labeled "The Lucky Landlord."

THIS WAS MY "LUCKY" ROUTINE

- Prospecting for properties
- Lining up investors and partners
- Daily thank-you notes for a year
- Thousands of calls and negotiations
- Networking with brokers, owners, and bankers

As I explained the property game to friends, my eyes not only opened to a future in real estate, the initial research for this book took shape. It seemed logical that entrepreneurial thinking I was learning on the streets might be as valuable as any other career course. Not real estate per se, but why weren't students taught basic networking, team building, negotiation strategies, project management, decision making, and the subtle art of thank-you notes?

Why wasn't there a Life-101 course for undergraduates? Were the experts hiding something? Get me the University president — I'm blowing this story wide open! But I digress. I was 19, full of passion and conspiracy theories.

Maybe the condo was dumb luck and I still had a lot to learn ...

Chapter 5
Extra Credit or Class Dismissed

> *"Wisdom is not a product of schooling*
> *but the lifelong attempt to acquire it."*
> ALBERT EINSTEIN (1879 – 1955)
> German-Swiss Theoretical Physicist

Who Me, a Boat Rocker?

A S A SOPHOMORE, I dreamed of attending USC's entrepreneur program, one of the best in the country. Before business school however, I had to knock out undergraduate courses. I loved history, cinema, philosophy, creative writing, and political science. On the flipside, prerequisite work for business school included calculus, statistics, and economics. How can I put this delicately? Just shoot me now — I'm semi-dyslexic! Although high finance is a noble pursuit and my apologies to spreadsheet lovers, we all had classes that tortured our souls. For me, it was any course that included math or financial theories.

"Bueller... Bueller ... Anyone ... Anyone ... Voodoo Economics?"

So I was thinking — if a student is fortunate enough to attend a top MBA or entrepreneur program such as those at USC or Harvard, the experience can be extraordinary. Courses at elite schools provide real-world lessons for students to sink their teeth into; they even teach some *Essentials* in this book. Alumni networks are also a genuine leg-up. The problem is most students in the real world never have the grades, money, or opportunity to attend such programs. I for one had two strikes against me — little patience and dwindling funds. The third curve ball was prerequisite math. It was like telling a science major he had to take prerequisite baseball — Strike Three!

So I started talking to friends with graduate degrees. Many I spoke with were in debt to their eyeballs and stressed out. Only a small percentage balanced the work-play thing. Most were changing careers before 30. Others felt their degree was a step in the door, but just as many never entered a profession for which their degree was required. Sufficiently freaking out, I began a bout with insomnia.

Around this time, I was sitting in the school cafeteria and overheard a casual debate among students and professors. They were discussing prerequisite courses and skyrocketing tuition costs. At one point, the dialogue fixated on a key question; "Do undergraduate and graduate programs offer enough real-world essentials?" With that, my ears perked up. I chimed in to ask if anyone cared to make this a weekly coffee talk. About five of us became regulars, mostly aspiring business majors. We saw ourselves as boat rockers — maybe we could change the education system? Our talks continued for months. Before long, we roped in everyone from freshman to seniors in myriad fields of study. By the end of my sophomore year, these Socratic chats on campus lawns got very interesting, maybe even a bit confrontational.

Many students felt a business degree was a ticket to success. Others valued liberal arts or their chosen field. Either way, we all agreed there were huge gaps in the system — like those heavy tuition costs and long semesters that didn't favor attention-deficit kids. We felt business programs placed too much emphasis on left-brain courses like statistics and accounting; missing the opportunity to better engage creative, right-brain students. We also questioned whether anyone was teaching basic success principles in science, music, or athletic programs.

So I asked my economics professor if I could conduct an extra-credit experiment. The idea was to survey a broad range of students and professionals from artists and athletes to CEOs and educators. I asked participants to rank factors they would use to evaluate employees and entrepreneurs alike; everything from grades and degrees to skills and personality traits. Ultimately, I was looking for common threads to success in life *and* business.

TITLE OF MY RESEARCH
Real-World Essentials Critical to Success

Fast-forward ninety days for survey results » A focus group of nearly 300 respondents indicated grades and graduate degrees were highly relevant assets, certainly indicators of hard work, and important to many employers. Chalk up points for higher education. However, grades and degrees weren't rated higher, and in many cases lower than: passion, experience, and work ethics. Among the highest-rated assets were teamwork and leadership abilities. Focus, problem solving, and creative-thinking skills were high on the list, along with communication and people skills. The most relevant values were integrity, humility, respect, and gratitude. In short, the survey validated that many *Essentials* were absent from college *and* corporate-training programs, especially undergraduate courses where students were most vulnerable. For my ambitious, teenage mind, these results begged two questions:

1 If success is determined in large part by certain *Essentials*, didn't logic dictate we teach these principles at the earliest, possible age?

2 Wouldn't teaching these *Essentials* improve confidence, grades, and performance; translating into greater success *and* happiness?

Final Grade

As my sophomore year was ending, I approached my professor to share results. I had my stats; even one of those fancy pie charts. My professor's first reaction was positive. He even agreed with my theory on *Essential* gaps in education. However, he was quick to point out that students could only learn so much from school and that surveys only tell a fraction of the story. "Some things can't be taught, Cliff. Many of life's abilities are gifts at birth or learned through experience," he said.

I agreed in part with my professor. "However," I said. "The idea that we always learn from experience is a total cliché. How do you explain intelligent people who repeat the same mistakes with years of *experience?*"

No response from my professor. I think he felt I was being disrespectful. At 19, I probably was. The point I hoped to make was that not everyone learns from a negative experience because they weren't taught to do so. Confidence may not have been instilled at home or in a classroom. Admitting failure, acknowledging shortcomings, or asking for help were not success strategies everyone was taught, but these are the master humility principles of mentors like Edison, Einstein, and Socrates. Sadly, many students succumb to peer pressure and learn poor habits in disorganized workplaces. Add physical challenges or a dysfunctional home life to the equation and all bets are off. "There's a good reason people don't learn from experience, Professor." That's what I was trying to say anyway.

Looking at so many variables, it was clear not everyone learns *how to learn* from experience (especially at a young age). Many talented people get frustrated after a negative experience. They become gun-shy after mistakes, failing to try new things. They might even become *less experienced* as they age.

At best, many of us were given broken pieces to this huge puzzle but never shown the whole picture.

My Radical Theory > Experience doesn't inherently teach success principles. At best, we often learn what not to do. However, avoiding bad habits is not the same as learning *Essentials* for a competitive environment. Therefore, the most basic skills, strategies, and values must be essential to a quality education in *any* field of study.

So I asked my professor if he wanted to join our coffee talks. He smiled, encouraged my research, and left the room. Then I glanced at the chalkboard where a popular business lesson was etched in big letters — **Opportunity Cost** — *the value of selecting one opportunity instead of another.*

I took a few minutes to calculate the cost of staying in college (years and money). I then walked off campus, never to return as a student. Admittedly, it was an impulsive thing to do. I had never quit anything and regretted the decision years later. I could have learned so much more, met so many amazing people, and benefitted from countless opportunities in the most rewarding setting of my life; a college campus. Truth is, I loved school. I would never recommend anyone leave if they had the means or motive to enjoy the experience.

Sadly, I couldn't afford to stay. Insomnia and an empty wallet sent me packing. Still, I learned a lot at USC, even from professors I disagreed with. I was just too young to appreciate it. In the end, a healthy debate took place between us misfits and the establishment — I think that was a good thing.

For me, it all boiled down to a few simple questions: what are we learning, when should we learn it, and how do we ensure optimal readiness for every student or professional?

I was now convinced more than ever that connecting *Essentials* like entrepreneurial thinking was critical to success. So I walked away from USC intimidated by what I had bargained for, but hopeful my college experience would serve as a real-world MBA; my **M**aster's in **B**asic **A**bilities. Like most 20-year-old kids, I didn't always make decisions with a clear head or bigger vision. I hadn't learned *The 4th Essential* yet (purpose). I was young and naive; still in survival mode. I lacked humility. A few things were clear though — 9 to 5 wasn't my speed and my entrepreneurial soul was itching to unleash. Armed with my little condo and a half-baked success survey, it was time to put my radical theory to the test.

Hello scary world. Here I come ...

Chapter 6
Welcome to The Real World

> *"Small opportunities are often
> the beginning of great enterprises."*
> DEMOSTHENES (384 – 322 BC)
> Greek Statesman, Orator

Flying High

IN 1988, I TURNED 21. I had no safety net if my real estate gig didn't work out. Fortunately, I walked smack into the real-estate boom of the late '80s. It was time to sell the condo. I was fortunate to sell at the height of the market, pay off Bill, and experience my first win. I felt like the luckiest kid on the planet so I didn't spend a dime on myself. Instead, I parlayed profits into two more houses.

I hired contractors and started remodeling. I soon learned about little things that could go wrong; like plumbing and electrical problems, or sub-contractors taking twice as long and costing three times more than promised. Rain delays and city inspectors screwed up perfectly-planned schedules too. Nonetheless, I survived. Improving on my college formula, I simply applied my advanced calculus skills and bought homes with extra bedrooms. The logic > more rooms = more rental income. I kept a master suite for myself and stretched every dollar to generate real cash flow for the first time in my life.

Since the properties were working out, I studied at night and earned my real estate license. With years of street practice under my belt, I went to work for a prominent residential broker. I was hardly a rookie after college so I assumed I could handle it all — I went full tilt as a realtor, investor, and mortgage guy. I helped friends buy houses and negotiated their loans too. Even the guys I chased properties with as a college freshman became clients. Those thank-you notes never stopped paying off.

Within a few years, I had purchased three more properties. I was a 22-year-old millionaire, livin' the dream (on paper anyway). Then, in the Fall of '89, the real estate market crashed. It took me a while to realize the storm I was in. By the Summer of '90, I was in over my head with vacancies and expensive contractors. I had to sell each property and my savings were wiped out. Five years of blood, sweat, and tears went down the drain in just a few months.

Welcome to the real world, big shot!

Youthful Lessons Learned

It was a painful experience but the '89 real estate crash taught me valuable lessons — Realtor? Mortgage guy? Investor? Landlord? Remodeling junkie? Dude, you have to focus! In the '80s, everyone bit off more than they could chew. I was no different. I saw many friends repeat the same mistakes in the '90s and 2000s. Nonetheless, I was still a young pup in '91. I loved real estate and was eager to start my own company. Friends told me I was nuts to think about opening my own firm in a bad market; but if ignorance was bliss, I was ecstatic. I had no business plan or much cash left, but I understood a few *Essentials*:

1 Show up daily.
2 Provide great service.
3 Express sincere gratitude.
4 Make more money than you spend.
5 Work ass off. Lather. Rinse. Repeat.

It wasn't the textbook success formula we learned in school but my basic abilities served me well. I was wiped out financially, but I had something of greater value than cash. I had a trusted reputation. Referrals were also very consistent by now. In my gut I thought, "Why not start a business — if times are bad, won't people need help?" That naiveté was a good thing. Sometimes, you have to ignore the critics who say it can't be done, then take a leap of faith.

So in 1991, age 24, I leaped ...

Think Big or Die Hard

*"Never be afraid to ask for too much
when selling or offer too little when buying."*
WARREN BUFFETT (1930 –)
American Industrialist, Philanthropist

If buying my first condo in college was a stroke of luck, then negotiating my first office space was a bowl of Lucky Charms. Picture the Fox Plaza on Avenue of the Stars, one of the most luxurious buildings in Century City, Los Angeles. You might recognize this skyscraper from the 1988 Bruce Willis movie, *Die Hard* (Nakatomi Plaza for you movie buffs). It was the ultimate location to entertain clients, bankers, and fellow brokers. Lucky me, I scored prime space in that building with city views at just $400 per month — but if I'm telling the whole story, it was basically free. Ready for the secret?

About this time, I had lunch each week with a lawyer named Kim. I bought sushi and Kim mentored me in negotiation strategies. The topic one day was old-fashioned barter. Kim suggested I make an offer to sublease a small office inside the nicest building I could find, then trade my services in exchange for free rent. I thought Kim was nuts with this pro-bono stuff but I gave it a shot. I called everyone I knew, including some leasing agents in Beverly Hills. Within a month, a real estate attorney named Dave heard my proposal through the grapevine. As it turned out, Dave represented one of my clients who vouched for me. So far, so good.

Dave told me he had just signed a lease for 10,000 square feet in the Fox Plaza. Unfortunately, the merger of his 3-man law firm to a big corporation fell apart. He was stuck with all that space! Fortunately for me, Dave was into real estate. I told him I was opening a firm on a slim budget, but would provide pro-bono services in exchange for a tiny wing of free office space. With nothing to lose, I also asked if I could use the phones, copiers, leather chairs, and mahogany desks that were collecting dust. Dave never blinked. He said, "Okay Cliff. I like you and I buy real estate. As my broker, you can save me commissions and serve as my chief negotiator. Offer some free mortgages for my staff and you have a deal — but I have to charge $400 for parking spaces, okay?" I grinned, shook his hand, and said, "I can live with that." In my head I was thinking, "Holy crap, what did I just pull off?"

Risking little cash and getting that killer space with all the freebies was like a Vegas jackpot for a startup company. With money saved, I hired an assistant, attracted a few salespeople, and began working around the clock. The occasional freebie for Dave and his colleagues was no skin off my nose. I was getting plenty of referrals networking in the hottest building in town. I also asked Dave if he'd allow me to sublease a few desks to agents. There was so much empty space, he agreed. Within a month, I was turning a small profit on the sublease alone. From then on, I never neglected to ask for exactly what I wanted in negotiations. The worst anyone ever said was, "No."

Work + Gratitude = Results

In 1992, Cliff Michaels & Associates opened as a boutique real estate and mortgage firm in the Fox Plaza. We handled mostly residential estates and a few commercial deals. My first upscale clients were referred by my accountant, Michael Shillan. Michael was the big brother who took a chance on me; a wet-behind-the-ears entrepreneur. Other financial advisors in those early years were Harley Neuman and John Halperin. Thanks again, Michael, Harley, and John for sage advice and countless referrals.

In the beginning, I cranked out calls from morning to midnight and obsessed over clients. I soon gained a reputation as a tough negotiator; mostly due to a little secret I gleaned from a street-wise mentor — I often warmed up the other side with gift baskets as I hammered away at price, terms, and conditions. I learned early in the game that people are friendlier with a box of chocolate muffins or bottle of wine on their desk.

During transactions, I would conference clients with their financial team, then review negotiations points. If a deal didn't feel right, I advised against it. I often spent months helping clients clean up bad credit. The financial advisors who handled high-profile clients liked that I was never desperate to do a deal. They also appreciated my confidentiality policy. Many brokers made a living calling media each time a famous client was involved. I preferred to be the confidant behind the entourage. Before long, business managers trusted me because I cared more about a client's privacy than my commissions or self-promotion.

Within three years, referrals were flooding my office. My small team and I closed hundreds of mortgages and tens of millions of dollars in property sales annually. The idea of building a big company never appealed to me. I was having a blast with a small, but highly profitable business. Friends with large organizations had a million headaches. That was the lifestyle I wanted to avoid.

By 27, that penniless soccer kid from the Valley now had a thriving real estate biz. What fascinated friends was how I was getting so many deals without advertising. Even competitors would look at the stack of deals on my desk and know I was doing just fine. With average homes in West Los Angeles starting at $500,000 dollars back then, even small deals provided healthy commissions.

To me, thriving in competitive waters wasn't complicated. I wasn't smarter and didn't have a big-name firm. I just worked hard and treated clients like family. Each time a deal closed, I sent gifts and thank-you cards. Then I invited the client's entourage to lunch. The agents in turn referred friends and peers. Managers referred accountants and lawyers. Everyone had a stock broker. It was quite the merry-go-round. My best secret (if I had one) was tipping the delivery guy $5 to parade gift baskets around a client's office, singing, "Delivery from Cliff Michaels and Associates — plenty of muffins and cookies for everyone!"

Before long, a few colleagues caught on to my tricks and asked if I would train their sales teams. "Why not?" I thought. How hard could it be to teach the magic of muffin marketing and thank-you notes? From college days as the Hershey-Kisses Kid, I became Muffin-Marketing Michaels.

My lessons as a sales trainer were simple too: consistent networking, daily follow-up, and strong relationships through gratitude. My cardinal rule — *Never leave your desk until you've written 5 thank-you notes per day*. I added negotiation workshops to the mix and suddenly I had a consulting business. Who knew my real estate buddies didn't learn this stuff in school either?

By 1996, my firm had closed a few hundred million dollars in sales. I never bought fancy clothes or lived an extravagant life. I was a jeans-and-t-shirt guy, dating, having fun, living a simple life in Los Angeles. But at 29, bouts with insomnia returned. I was suffering from burnout as my morning-to-midnight routine caught up with me. Physically I was fine. I played tennis, hit the gym, and had a healthy lifestyle. Mentally, I was toast. I finally asked colleagues to cover for me. It was time for a long-overdue sabbatical.

Hello Golf Coach and Travel Agent

For the next year, I traveled, took golf lessons, and hung out at country clubs. I was a natural golfer (at the range). On the course, I was a bit dangerous to fellow duffers (thankfully, no damage done).

Better use of time was spent mentoring high-school kids and college entrepreneurs. Each week, I took some time to teach sales, negotiations, and remodeling strategies to aspiring students. In turn, these quasi-interns assisted my sales agents. This gave me time to explore new ideas for life and business. By now I had dumped the fancy office in the Fox Plaza. It served it's purpose as a start-up location; but the novelty of going up and down 24 floors every day soon wore off. I moved back to the Valley to be closer to friends and my two sisters. My real estate team and I went virtual and worked from home. Who needs an office with computers and e-mail?

About this time, I met Nancy, a beautiful girl with a warm smile and kind heart. We met at a health club and were smitten from day one with a common love for travel, fitness, and the great outdoors. We soon took a road trip up the California coastline and spent a week in Big Sur with my sisters and their husbands. Big Sur is where ocean and water falls meet the redwoods in Northern California. Good medicine for restless souls. This sanctuary became one of my favorite getaway spots for contemplating life and chillin' out.

Nancy and I dated a while after that first trip to Big Sur and were happy campers. We hit the social scene in Los Angeles and enjoyed the good life. As much fun as we were having though, the 20-something gypsy in each of us wasn't ready to settle down. We were still searching for new adventures.

As for me, my creative soul had vacationed too long. After a year of golf, dating, and brainstorming, I was crawling the entrepreneurial walls of my mind. This new toy called *The Internet* was catching on. I wasn't a computer guy, but maybe the World Wide Web could scratch my itch for innovation.

I didn't understand the high-tech lingo but my sister Gigi sure did. She was into Web mania before most people had an e-mail address. It was Gigi who schooled me on finer points of the Internet scuttlebutt.

Dot-com? Dot what? So much for a life of leisure ...

Chapter 7
Diary of a Dot-com

> *"Business opportunities are like buses ...*
> *There's always another one coming."*
> RICHARD BRANSON (1950 –)
> British Entrepreneur, Adventurer, Philanthropist

Preamble

In 2001, I wrote a book titled, *Diary of a Dot-com*. It chronicled the true, roller-coaster ride of an Internet startup called FirstUse.com. It was also the wildest business risk of my life. I never published the original 50,000-word story. I'll explain why in a bit. You're about to read the 14-page, high-octane edition.

The adventure began just before launching my first Internet company in the '90s. I had recently been invited to join the Young Entrepreneurs' Organization (YEO), one of the world's premier networks for peer-to-peer learning among business owners (known today as the Entrepreneurs' Organization — EO).

By 2011, EO had grown to 8000 members, with over 120 chapters in 40 countries. I sat on the Los Angeles board from 1995 to 2004 and was honored to serve as chapter President in 2003/2004. When I joined this group of fellow risk-takers, I was constantly humbled by new ideas and fast-growth strategies around the globe. All I ever did was buy and sell real estate in Los Angeles. Clearly, there was more to life; maybe even different paths to success.

I had no sooner attended a YEO Global Leadership Conference when my peers challenged me to think bigger! "You're a passionate guy, Cliff — why not jump online and build a billion-dollar business? Change the world!"

Sounded good to me. Fasten your seat belt ...

Hatching an Idea

I ALWAYS WANTED TO do something related to my college research on success principles. The Internet seemed like a perfect venue, so in 1996 I designed a series of training programs for entrepreneurs and launched a website called Knowledge Café. I thought I would carve out a niche for myself and compete with this crazy company called Amazon.com. If they could sell books, why couldn't I sell audio programs and build a community for young entrepreneurs? Like I said, I didn't understand the Internet thing when it started. I assumed Amazon.com was just a fad.

Reality check aside, Knowledge Café gained a small following and made a few dollars thanks to a cool web design by my sister, Gigi. She and her husband, Craig Honick, were building e-commerce sites as early as 1994. So just as I was ramping up Knowledge Café, I got a late-night call from Craig that piqued my Web interest further. The dialogue went something like this ...

Agoura Hills, California, Winter, 1996

Rrrrrring ... Rrrrrring ...

CLIFF: "Midnight? Who goes there?"

CRAIG: "Cliff, it's Craig. You asleep?"

CLIFF: "Dozing off. What's up?"

CRAIG: "Come over."

CLIFF: "Really buddy? It's sleepy time."

CRAIG: "Sleep is for wimps. Come over. We have sushi and brownies. Oh, and I have a billion-dollar idea. Let's chat."

CLIFF: "Sushi and brownies? On my way." Twenty minutes later, I arrived at Craig and Gigi's house. "Mmmm, half-baked brownies! So what's the big idea?"

CRAIG: "I've been building a website for a lawyer in London. He's paranoid about Internet thieves stealing client logos and computer files online. He wanted to know if web developers had a method to register *first use* of web pages and design work before posting stuff on the Web."

CLIFF: "You mean like copyrights and trademarks — isn't that his expertise?"

CRAIG: "Yes, but there's a challenge. There will soon be millions of websites. Maybe a billion Internet users one day. Individuals and companies are going online in a big way — music, video, banking, file sharing, corporate records. You name it. Most people, especially lawyers, are clueless about cyberspace."

CLIFF: "Interesting. More sushi?"

CRAIG: "Most computers and online services enable people to create, share, and back up files, but there's a huge missing link."

CLIFF: "Your billion-dollar idea is the missing link? Tell me more, Darwin." I was such a non-techie that most of what Craig was saying went over my head.

CRAIG: "Hypothetically, if you wrote a will, screenplay, business plan, or software code, and wanted irrefutable evidence of what you created and when, how would you do it?"

CLIFF: "Hmm. Copyright? Patent? Keep a log book? Have the work notarized? Someone once told me to mail myself a date-stamped certified letter; leaving the envelope sealed in case I ever had to prove the creation date. How's that?"

CRAIG: "Not bad, but even notarized documents can be tampered with. An inventor can doctor his own logbook. Things are even more precarious in cyberspace — everyone has the means and motive to backdate digital files. Any document can be altered seconds after it's been created. In short, the chain of evidence for electronic records inherently lacks trust. Get it?"

CLIFF: "*Very Interesting*. More brownies? So what's the billion-dollar idea?

CRAIG: "The idea is this — there are zillions of documents on computers. Think of all the content going online. Now imagine a trusted registry on the Internet that could instantly timestamp and authenticate the world's files the moment they're created. Then imagine the ability to instantly resolve disputes if the origin or integrity of those records were ever challenged.

CLIFF: "Zillions of documents? A registry for time-stamping? How the heck do we do that?"

CRAIG: "Not sure. Still working on the idea. Cool if we could do it though. Don't ya think?

At the time, Craig was a college professor teaching economics at Cal State Northridge. He was also working on his Ph.D at UCLA — his research was based on Organizational Change. His understanding of business cycles and Internet trends was extraordinary. His idea for a time-stamping registry was on a collision course with the Internet boom.

In 1996, analysts projected 250,000,000 personal computers by 2000. There were 2 billion Internet users by 2011. Facebook alone was closing in on a billion users when I wrote this book. Can anyone fathom the number of files on world computers? How about all the websites and intellectual property? Is *zillions* even a word? Back then, Craig's idea was revolutionary. I was so inspired, I scrapped Knowledge Café to focus on the registry idea. I could always come back to writing and training entrepreneurs.

I remember the night Craig pitched the idea to me. "Imagine if each client only spent $10 and registered just one file?" I grabbed a calculator and punched in a few numbers based on projected Internet users. I showed it to Craig. We laughed. The numbers were too big! Maybe we should only charge $.99 cents per file? What if companies could privately register proof of e-mails and corporate records each day for pennies per file or a flat subscription fee for bulk files? Any way we sliced it, this wasn't a million-dollar idea. It was a billion-dollar monster!

Like most dot-com virgins, the fact that neither of us had run a technology company never phased us. This was one of those ideas that felt like one-in-a-billion. So we considered the famous tandems of technology: Filo and Yang (Yahoo), Gates and Allen (Microsoft), Jobs and Wosniak (Apple). Could Honick and Michaels be on to the next big thing?

After our midnight sushi and brownie fest, we made a pact to meet in the evenings and noodle ideas about the registry. If we ever got this company off the ground, my role was to raise capital and drive marketing. Craig was going to design the website and handle the tech side of things.

Were we about to become Co-CEOs in the Wild, Wild, West of the World Wide Web? In our minds, we already had.

Recap of the Global Challenge (then and now)

1 All digital records can be easily altered and backdated.
2 The World Wide Web is the ultimate copy machine.
3 Theft and infringement are at all-time highs and growing.
4 Computer networks enable instant distribution worldwide.
5 The legal process for disputes is slow and expensive.
6 Laws and language vary country to country.
7 With open networks, who can be trusted to keep honest records?

The Solution

We called the company FirstUse.com (First Use). It was the world's first online registry for trusted time-stamping and authentication of digital records. Our process enabled users to browse their computer, select a file, then create a time-sealed chain of evidence for creative work or important records.

How Did the Registry Work?

Let's say you're creating a digital file (song, video, screenplay, software code, or legal document). The first step is to save the file on your computer, right? Now imagine you could click one more button that enables you to confidentially *time-seal and register* that file with FirstUse.com. *(Once fully developed, FirstUse.com could plug into virtually any software program; e.g. Microsoft).*

Microsoft Word File
New
Open ...
Close ...
Save
Save As ...
Time-Stamp FirstUse.com
Verify with FirstUse.com
Page Setup
Print Preview
Print

What could be registered?

First Use enabled users to authenticate any size or type of electronic record from text and audio to video and photos. The beauty of our system was that no one at First Use could ever see a user's file. First Use would only store a time-stamped record of a file's digital fingerprint ...

Sample Digital Fingerprint
STDNF_1_65a373rp754tfz007gk54fdgdd

A digital fingerprint is known in tech-talk as a *one-way hash code*. It can be generated by applying an algorithmic formula to a file's binary code (the zeros and ones that make up digital files). No two files will generate the same digital fingerprint. Much like a human fingerprint is unique to each person, First Use could match any computer file with a unique digital fingerprint, then attach the fingerprint to a secure timestamp. First Use would then store the time-stamped fingerprint along with a user's account information. Storing billions of digital records is done the same way banks do it (with high-tech back-up and security measures). The process was seamless to customers who just had to visit FirstUse.com to set up an account, select a file, then click one button to time-stamp and register.

A FIRST USE REGISTRATION CERTIFICATE
WAS STORED AND E-MAILED TO THE CLIENT.

FirstUse.com

Time-Stamped Registration and Authentication Certificate

Registrant: John Doe
Address: 123 Dream Idea Lane
Los Angeles, California, 90049

File Name: Killer Screenplay
File #: 6547564765
Digital Fingerprint: 65*373*754!&0075454

Date: 12/5/96
Time of Registration: 12:42:30 a.m. GMT

"CONFIDENTIAL. SIMPLE. SECURE ... SO YOU CAN PROVE IT."

Mathematics and The Law — A Universal Standard

Because the world is made up of many laws and languages, there is only one universal language for resolving disputes — the language of mathematics. All legal cases boil down to testimony or trusted evidence. In the case of First Use, the dispute resolution process would be mathematically certain. In layman's terms, our system for digital authentication and time-stamping was as trustworthy, if not more so, than any other in the world.

The Value Proposition

Files could be registered and verified 24/7. At a few dollars per file, or pennies per file for corporate users, First Use was easier, faster, and less expensive than traditional evidence like $10 notaries, $20 copyrights, or expensive trademarks and patents. First Use wasn't a substitute for notaries or government-registered intellectual property, but a critical audit trail in case of disputes. Moreover, First Use provided something far more valuable — instantaneous and tamperproof evidence of what you created, when you created it, and that files had never been altered after the fact.

Pre-Launch Preparation

Starting in 1997, Craig and I spent nearly two years on research and development. We started with a visit to my attorney, Jay Patel, to see if the legal strength of First Use was as significant as we thought. As we described the registry idea, Jay looked at us as if we had discovered plutonium. "If you guys can do what you think you can, raise a truckload of capital and do it fast," said Jay. We soon talked with dozens of top lawyers at the most prominent law firms in the world. Most lawyers said the same thing as Jay. "If you build it, they will come."

The Business Plan

To raise venture capital, we knew a plan of this magnitude required heavy due diligence in technology law, development costs, and secure time-stamping. Craig and I had busy lives by day so at night we turned into research machines. A hundred drafts and eighteen months later, the First Use business plan was done. It was now 1998.

Along the way, we consulted experts who knew about complex web and software development. One of them was a pal of mine, Tony East. Tony is one of those math wizards like Matt Damon's character in *Good Will Hunting* — software code was child's play. The good news, according to Tony, was our instincts were right. What we wanted to build was relatively easy. The bad news? If we could easily do it, so could someone else. Wouldn't that suck if someone beat us to the punch?

They Did? Are You F*@#ing Kidding Me?

The funny thing about business plans is they're only good until you start a company. Then all bets are off and you better think on your feet. As a result of our research, we unearthed a little-known, patented technology that originated in the early '90s at Bellcore Labs (a spin-off of AT&T). The technology was subsequently marketed by a company called Surety Technologies. Guess what it was called? Digital Notary! It provided the most tamperproof and cryptographically secure time-stamping in the world.

Surety was doing very little business and no one we talked to had even heard of them. On the other hand, our Chief Tech Guru Tony suggested that Surety was not only a competitive threat but we might be infringing on their patents if we continued with our current business plan.

Although the wind was temporarily pulled from our sails, we wondered if there might be an opportunity to license Digital Notary. With nothing to lose, Craig and I cold-called Surety. We described First Use in basic terms. Ironically, Surety didn't see us as a threat to their primary customer target — big corporations. We were so far below their radar, they considered us more of a novelty for creative artists. In their view, we were a perfect partner to show off Digital Notary to consumers. In reality, we were invading their turf. We intended to start with individuals; making Digital Notary accessible to every Internet user in the world, then add features to make it easy for big corporations too.

We soon jumped on a plane to visit Surety at their headquarters in New Jersey. Their offices were huge but empty. Their management team was friendly but their marketing material would have confused Einstein, let alone Average Joe. After just one face-to-face meeting, Surety was so impressed with the simplicity of FirstUse.com, they granted us rights to plug Digital Notary into our online registry. If we succeeded, they would gain from the small licensing fee they charged us. If we failed, no skin off anyone's nose. Win-win.

Money Time

Plugging in Surety's Digital Notary probably saved us a year of development time and a fortune in startup costs. Digital Notary also gave us instant credibility with lawyers and technology folks who wondered how tamperproof our system would be. For those who appreciated secure technology, the alliance with Surety was either dumb luck or a stroke of genius. There was only one thing left to do — raise capital!

Craig and I began dialing for dollars. Our plan called for at least $300,000 just to launch (legal, marketing, employees, office space, web development, software developers, back-up systems). Ultimately, we needed millions of dollars for the business plan we structured.

We first considered venture capitalists (VCs). At this stage, a typical VC would likely want control of First Use and a heavy pound of flesh. Many young entrepreneurs lose their companies by getting into bed too early with the wrong VC. We didn't want to make a mistake. Having said that, the right VC can be worth their weight in sales, alliances, public relations, future capital, and management wisdom. Our goal was to hit the big VCs once we launched and had some leverage.

As cool as the idea was, the world still needed an education about First Use as the de facto registry for authenticating digital records. We also had to explain our hip technology and elements of law. No easy task. Clearly, the fastest route for startup capital would have to be angels (friends or high-net-worth investors). Since we didn't come from wealthy families, our Rolodexes and reputations would have to lead the way. We knew the road ahead was tough, but we also believed First Use was a huge solution to a global challenge. Someone would surely see our vision.

Of the countless investors we spoke to in 1998, most people thought the registry was brilliant but too risky for seed capital. Finally, two gentlemen were as passionate about our plan as we were. Their names were Gordy Brown and Neil Paolella. After reading our plan, seeing the website, and hosting a series of meetings, Gordy and Neil were in.

Craig and I were excited about our angels, Gordy and Neil. First, and respectfully, they added gray hairs and wisdom. Gordy was the Founder of Your Staff, a $100 million-dollar company and pioneer in the employee-leasing business, now a multibillion-dollar industry. Neil, an investment banker, helped Gordy sell Your Staff to a major competitor. These were real-world experiences Craig and I didn't have.

By now, friends had watched us labor nearly two years on the First Use plan. Craig was still working on his Ph.D at UCLA and teaching at CSUN. He and my sister Gigi were raising my niece Jenny, 12, and nephew Ryan, 9. I still had a successful real estate business, but was itching to build something again — if not another house, then a pioneering dot-com would suit me fine. I had already funded two years of legal, travel, and other expenses for First Use and we still needed to raise millions more. The consensus was clear. Take the $300,000 and launch this puppy already!

We met at Gordy's house for wine, signatures, and a toast to future success. Since less than 1% of angel-seeking entrepreneurs ever find capital, Craig and I were not only pumped, we were eternally grateful.

Game On

Capital in hand, we launched First Use near Westlake Village, California, in late 1998. We hired programmers, recruited salespeople, and began a PR campaign. Craig was a website-building machine, working with code developers around the clock. I kept chasing capital, handled press interviews, and worked on sales with our VP of Business Development, Mike Reid. Mike was a work horse with a seasoned background in Internet marketing; the kind of guy you want on a startup team.

Mike and I typically worked 16-hour days. Craig outpaced everyone; often working until 4:00 a.m. — to this day, I have no idea how he functioned on a few hours sleep each night. By launch time however, Craig had designed a stellar website. As for the crazy technology I'd never heard of before we started, it really worked! Most of the tech talk was beyond my comprehension but I soon memorized the jargon: hash codes, fingerprints, and encryption algorithms. It was all digital madness to me!

I also learned that technology can be riddled with bugs that burn cash and slow down development in ways you could never imagine. So much for my focus on sales. Within four months, my day job was chasing capital again. Welcome to the real-world of fast-growth, Internet startups. *Any entrepreneurs feeling my pain?*

Glitches and money issues aside, things were looking up. Mike recruited Christiane Hile, a multi-lingual lawyer with a sales background in high tech. We affectionately called her Chile and she was a rock-star from the word *go*. As we hit Internet conferences, Mike and Chile were signing strategic alliances left and right, mostly trade associations in legal, tech, and entertainment. This attracted early adopters like lawyers, techies, and creative artists. Educating the public about Digital Notary and the law remained tricky. It's one thing to have a solution for the world's digital trust and time-stamping issues. It's another explaining it. Keep in mind, it was 1999 — there was no Facebook or social media to get the word out. Still, a small part of the world was now discovering First Use.

FirstUse.com

Where the World Registers Ideas and Records
... So You Can Prove It

The Early Buzz

FirstUse.com Launches Global Time-Stamping Registry

Entrepreneur Magazine · Red Herring · Los Angeles Business Journal
Law Technology News · Los Angeles Times · Business 2.0
Success Magazine · Daily Variety · Forrester Research

By summer of '99, we had some press and real-world customers in 70 countries. The media attention was minor but for those playing in our sandbox, First Use was a fascinating global solution. A few VCs loved the idea but felt we were still too early to fetch big dollars. They also wanted to be sure First Use had the legal strength we claimed it did. Fair enough — we worked on that too.

Adding Legal Punch

To build credibility in public relations, we aligned with influential attorneys who understood our technology and real-world legal solution. Our general counsel was Andrew Sherman in Washington D.C., a top intellectual property lawyer with clients like AOL. Andrew was also a friend and general counsel to the Young Entrepreneurs' Organization — we met though YEO. Andrew was a First Use cheerleader from day one with sage advice and a powerful network. He made an early introduction to one of his colleagues in Los Angeles, entertainment lawyer, Susan Grode. Susan then introduced us to Meryl Marshall, Chairwoman for the Academy of Television Arts and Sciences. Meryl was also a former attorney who quickly understood First Use. She helped us form an alliance with the Academy and pitched us to writers, directors, and artists. With a little buzz from Academy members, it wasn't long before the Writer's Guild asked if First Use could somehow be plugged into their online registry plans.

As a result of early support from forward-thinking lawyers like Andrew, Susan, and Meryl, Craig and I were asked to speak at tech, legal, and Internet conferences from London to Los Angeles. We were the new kids on the block and audiences were genuinely fascinated. A small, but effective public relations campaign was now in full force.

Another star on our legal team was visionary attorney, Michael Brown, then a lawyer at Patton Boggs. Michael's father was Ron Brown, former Secretary of Commerce under President Clinton's administration. Michael knew everyone in Washington D.C. and saw the big picture of First Use. He soon put his political arm around us. Before long, Craig and I were invited to the White House.

Once there, Michael arranged for us to present First Use to technology advisors of President Bill Clinton and Vice President Al Gore. Michael also set up meetings with leaders of Congress, the Copyright office, and the Patent and Trademark office. Suffice to say, we were laying powerful ground work.

Still Chasing Dollars

The Internet was now moving at light speed and the danger of falling behind the technology curve was very real. Our revenue was less than expected and the cost of running First Use was growing. Goldman Sachs wasn't backing up the money truck just yet, so we continued to pursue private investors and small VCs. Anyone who has ever chased capital knows the drill — plenty of handshakes, load up your power point, and hope someone gets your mission.

There was constant interest in First Use but big VCs still weren't pulling the trigger. They wanted us to prove ourselves a bit more. Nonetheless, we raised nearly $3 million dollars in capital by the end of 1999. The money came in waves; one small VC invested $500,000, and dozens of private investors chipped in $25,000 to $250,000 each. As it turned out, we would need every penny. Technology and marketing costs were burning capital in ways we couldn't fathom. Craig, Mike, Chile and I would even forego salaries to ensure that web and software development didn't slow down. No big deal. We were confident the hard work in 1999 was about to pay off big in 2000.

Year-1 Recap

From global launch to pitching ideas in the White House, 1999 was a crazy year. It was also a huge learning experience for Craig and me. It took us a while to find our voice but once when we did, VCs started calling. They could see we had customers around the world and endorsements from media, legal, and technology experts. The big question: "Could First Use deliver to large corporations the way it had successfully appealed to small consumers?" Answer: "Yes." Our goal was to go after big companies once we proved how easy First Use could work for Average Joe.

"Okay," said the VCs. "How soon can you deliver the corporate edition of First Use?" Craig figured it would take another 6 to 12 to months to wrap up applications that could plug FirstUse.com into some of the world's most popular software programs and emerging tools for digital rights management. We also had plans to make things easy for companies to authenticate big batches of e-mails, corporate records, and web-based transactions. These upgrades to our strategy were mission-critical to VCs.

January 2000 ... A Cliffhanger

In spite of all the momentum and capital raised in 1999, we were running on financial fumes by early 2000. Our investors were incredibly supportive, but staked us as far as they could. The writing was now on the proverbial wall. We had to raise a war chest of capital, merge with a big company, or become a statistic in the world of failed dot-coms.

Craig and I fired up the dog-and-pony show one more time, pitching every VC who would listen. We soon attracted a venture arm of Ernst & Young (EY), one of the most recognized names in global consulting. The EY guys had seen Craig and me speak at several conferences and were impressed with First Use. With EY looking under our hood, major technology companies were now taking notice. One of them was RSA, the world leader in encryption algorithms. RSA is well known for spinning off Verisign, a world leader in authentication services.

Finally, in January, 2000, I got a call from one of our board advisors. He whispered, "Ernst & Young loves First Use — they want to fund your company." I ran into Craig's office and gave him a big hug. "Big money coming!" I shouted.

Within weeks, we had another offer from a Silicon Valley VC who not only offered capital, but discussed RSA as a potential partner. With multiple offers from different parties, we now had leverage. Initial offers included up to $5 million dollars in capital. First Use was potentially valued between $15 and $20 million. We were even told our company might be worth $50 million if we hit 12-month revenue projections. Could a billion-dollar company be far off?

Spring 2000 ... Victory at Hand

EY was excited about our vision and became the frontrunner VC. They promised to put the full force of their global resources behind First Use. However, in those early months of 2000, there was a funky vibe around Internet companies raising capital. Did these Generation-X startups with little revenue really merit $20 to $100 million-dollar values, let alone a billion? Did the VCs take on too much risk, signing over $10 million-dollar seed checks to 20-something rookies?

Craig and I were on pins and needles as our lawyers negotiated term sheets from January to April. After years of blood, sweat, and tears, and millions of dollars invested, this was our moment. Suddenly, with little warning in the spring of 2000, the dot-com bubble burst, venture capital dried up, and deals were falling apart for thousands of companies from Wall Street to Silicon Valley. Week after week, month after month, dot-bomb replaced dot-com in headlines around the world.

And the Fairy-tale Ending for FirstUse.com?

EY was first to jump ship. Our saviors from Silicon Valley disappeared shortly thereafter. No glory. No headlines. Game over. Craig and I continued to fight the good fight all year. We made dozens of presentations in hopes of a merger, buyout, or more capital. We couldn't strike a deal — and without capital, we couldn't survive. First Use soon became little more than a fascinating footnote in the world of pioneering Internet solutions.

In the end, Craig and I remained good friends who shared a once-in-a-lifetime experience. First Use shared a similar fate to many companies with great ideas — a dollar short, and in this case, perhaps ahead of its time.

These days, a form of digital-notary technology is imbedded in many Web and software tools. So when Craig and I see the evolution of digital time-stamping, we look back, smile, and say, "Yep, we helped pioneer that industry in the '90s. It was a wild ride!"

Special Thanks

To everyone who believed in us, Craig and I were grateful for the opportunity. We still believe a time-stamping registry was the most universal solution to a global challenge. Perhaps this story will inspire a young entrepreneur to build a better mousetrap.

Good luck future enterprisers!

My Lessons From the Edge

By the time we launched, we had no idea the dot-com bubble would soon burst. In the end, we had a great idea. We raised millions. We built a strong team. We worked like madmen. We still failed. Life goes on.

Hindsight being 20-20, here's the summary for my Diary of a Dot-com...

What Worked

According to the experts, we did many things right at First Use. We wrote a well-researched plan and bootstrapped early development. This was enough to earn respect and raise millions in venture capital. We had the humility to bring in a seasoned board of advisors and experts in our field. We built a small, in-house team, outsourced developers, and started an effective public-relations campaign. Most importantly, we proved we could attract paying customers and real-world alliances.

What Didn't Work

Before we launched, Craig and I spent too much time trying to write the perfect business plan. Although we brought in great teams by 1999, we should have solicited more experience as far back as 1997. **Major Lessons Learned: 1.)** Never let perfect ruin good; **2.)** Surround yourself from the start with as much seasoned talent as possible.

Big ideas often require twice as much time, money, and effort as you think. Given the chaos of hi-tech startups, we failed to budget early dollars more efficiently and we didn't raise nearly enough capital for a venture as ambitious as First Use. Craig and I didn't lack humility though — we asked for help. We lacked a better understanding of costs, timetables, and contingency plans in a rapidly-changing environment. For that matter, so did most Internet founders.

On the marketing side, we failed to build a solid foundation in any single market so we never generated much revenue in any market. There's a good chance we may have succeeded had we focused on small consumers or big corporations, but not both at the same time. **Bonus Lessons Learned:** If you don't have focus, revenue, and happy customers, you won't have a viable business for long, no matter how much capital you raise.

Biggest Lesson Learned

First Use made me a stronger entrepreneur. My biggest lesson however wasn't about VCs or running a business. It was about self-awareness. When we first embarked on First Use, I loved the idea of pioneering something big and making a difference in the world. Within six months of startup however, I realized I wasn't doing something I loved. High-tech for me — who are we kidding? The mission in the end was rediscovering my passion and purpose.

Suddenly, life threw another curve ball …

Chapter 8
Finding Passion and Purpose

> *"The secret of success is constancy of purpose."*
> BENJAMIN DISRAELI (1804 – 1881)
> British Prime Minister, Literary Figure

Success Through Adversity

Like most entrepreneurs, failure was critical to personal growth. True success only came when I learned to balance work, play, and life's bag of tricks. After First Use, I was fortunate to still have a successful real estate and consulting business. Nonetheless, I'd worked to the brink of burnout once too often. I always battled insomnia and it would be years before I understood my dyslexic shortcomings. A bit more on that later.

By now, I was 33. It was time to think about what made me truly happy ...

Purpose Through Crisis and Change

As CRAIG AND I made a final effort to save First Use, our family suffered an even greater loss. In the Spring of 2000, my niece, Jenny, was killed in a car accident (two weeks shy of 16). Jenny was a beautiful girl, one-in-a-billion soul, and always made me laugh. Her brother Ryan (13 back then), survived the crash. Jenny's loss and a failing business were a lot to process at the same time. However, Jenny showed us the way.

At 13, Jenny had written a poem titled *Life*. The opening line was, "Stop. Take a breath. Set aside your life." Her words were profound. So I took a year off to reflect, travel, and practice yoga. Naturally, I thought about Jenny quite a bit. My entrepreneurial adventures could wait another day.

How We Moved On

After First Use and Jenny's loss, Craig and Gigi moved to Bainbridge Island in Washington. With heavy hearts, each of us found new purpose. Craig soon built a consulting firm called Sector Intelligence. His company produces custom research reports for a variety of industries. In 2003, He and Gigi had a son, Ian. My nephew Ryan graduated from American University in Washington D.C. with a Master's in Communication. So proud of him!

In 2001, I wrote a book titled *Diary of a Dot-com*. I had offers from publishers and turned them down. Publishing the First Use story during a family crisis didn't feel right. So I put the manuscript under my bed, knowing the lessons would fit the right book when my head was clear and the writing bug struck again.

As the dot-com bubble burst in 2000, the real estate market boomed. I returned to buying and selling homes for clients and myself. It was good occupational therapy.

By 2002, I started raising money for charities with a focus on education and underprivileged youth. Something felt really good about that. My fellow entrepreneurs and I also mentored students, mostly at USC and UCLA. Once we got the bug, we donated hundreds of hours each year to young entrepreneurs. Helping those eager to make their mark on the world inspired me to make social entrepreneurship (giving) a cornerstone of my life moving forward.

In 2003, I relocated my real estate office and remodeled a beautiful Cape Cod home in Brentwood, California. It became a great spot for charity events and hanging out with good friends. I lived in Brentwood five years; the first place I ever called home. Until then, I had moved every few years my whole life.

With the real estate market turning, I sold my Brentwood home in 2007 before the 2008 market crash — lucky me. I then moved to Santa Monica and took a short sabbatical to Southeast Asia. The hospitality of people from Thailand to Malaysia gave me a renewed sense of purpose and gratitude. In 2008, I outlined this book while vacationing on the island of Boracay in the Philippines. Something about white-sand beaches always gets me writing.

So there you have it — *My Lessons From the Edge* — a real-world degree I could never get in college. Turns out my professor back at USC was right all along; some things we only learn through experience.

Ready for Takeoff?

Now that you've heard my story, it's time to take you on a high-speed journey of your own. I'll do my best to guide you through *4 Essentials of Entrepreneurial Thinking* that I wish someone had shared with me sooner in life. As the saying goes, "If I only knew then what I know now."

Mostly, I hope lessons in this book help you learn, love, live, and give with passion, humility, and gratitude.

Here's to your amazing journey!

Cliff Michaels

Essential # 1: **Basic Life Skills**

"Being ignorant is not so much a shame, as being unwilling to learn."
BENJAMIN FRANKLIN (1706 – 1790)
American Politician, Author, Inventor

Getting Started

ALTHOUGH YOU CAN ALWAYS bounce around this book, if this is your first time through *The 4 Essentials*, it's best to read chapters in order.

Some sections will feel like essays. Others like blogs. Either way, enjoy the ride.

Skill 1   Define success.

Skill 2   Unleash your entrepreneurial soul.

Skill 3   Build a passion for learning.

Skill 4   Leverage tools and mentors.

Skill 5   Cultivate curiosity and creativity.

Skill 6   Practice with passion and purpose.

Skill 7   Never quit. Failure is your friend.

Skill 8   Embrace challenge and change.

Skill 9   Be ambitious but recognize greed.

Skill 10   Carpe diem, baby!

Skill 1
Define Success

> *"Success is liking yourself,*
> *liking what you do, and liking how you do it."*
> MAYA ANGELOU (1928 –)
> American Poet, Historian, Activist

What's your definition of the good life?

- World Peace
- Love and Laughter
- Art and Innovation
- Giving and Gratitude
- Fun · Friends · Family
- Money · Power · Fame
- A Healthy Mind · Body · Soul

Fifteen years before I wrote *The 4 Essentials*, a friend e-mailed me a popular fable about how we define success and happiness. Hybrids of the story floated on the Internet for decades. It's been written by countless poets in many languages with themes from pirate's tale to Buddhist myth. Curious to its modern origin, I discovered a German writer named Heinrich Böll (1917 – 1985). Böll, a Nobel Prize winner, wrote a parable in 1963 called "Anecdote to the Decline of the Work Ethic." It tells the tale of a traveling businessman who attempts to lecture a fisherman about success. Instead, the businessman learns a valuable lesson from the fisherman.

I next discovered a modern version of the fable titled, "The Mexican Fisherman," written in 1996 by Dr. Mark Albion. Mark is a fellow entrepreneur and former professor at Harvard Business School. In 2009, Mark re-titled "The Mexican Fisherman," calling it "The Good Life." When I told Mark about my book, he was gracious enough to let me put my spin on "The Good Life."

While *The 4 Essentials* is a series of my original essays, I couldn't think of a better way to start readers on a fun journey toward success.

Without further ado, here's my version of the famous fisherman's tale …

Harvard Joe and the Fisherman (adapted with permission from Dr. Mark Albion's *The Good Life*)

AFTER GRADUATING FROM HARVARD Business School, an American stock broker named Joe decided to take a vacation. He chose a small island, famous for its quiet fishing village and local smiles. If only to take his mind off business a few days, Joe vowed he would fish a little and avoid the money-talk so prevalent on Wall Street.

On his first day of vacation, Joe strolled along the beach. He spotted a small fishing boat coming into shore. Inside the boat were a lone fisherman and a fresh catch of large tunas. Dozens of locals and tourists were handing over cash as the fisherman docked his boat. Joe was so impressed, he complimented the fisherman and asked how long it took to catch so many fish.

"Not long at all," said the fisherman. "Plenty of fish in these waters."

"Why don't you stay out longer and catch more fish?" asked Joe. "You could certainly make more money in such rich waters."

The fisherman smiled and said, "Oh, I catch more than enough to support my family and lifestyle."

"But what do you do with the rest of your time?" asked Joe.

The fisherman replied, "I read, nap a bit, and play with my daughters. Some days I teach kids how to fish. Other days I play soccer with school children. In the afternoons, I stroll into the village where I sip wine and play guitar with my lovely wife and friends. Most nights we cook fish and share recipes with the tourists."

"Wow, you have loads of free time," said Joe. "Listen, I have an MBA. I can help you vastly expand your business. If you simply spend more time fishing, you would soon earn enough money to buy a bigger boat."

"Really?" asked the fisherman.

"Absolutely," said Joe. "And with a bigger boat, you could catch enough fish to buy several boats, then a whole fleet. At that point you would be successful enough to sell directly to a processor, cutting out the middleman, and vastly increasing your profits. Eventually, you could open your own cannery, controlling product and distribution!"

"Then what?" asked the fisherman.

"If all goes well, you'll find yourself in a big city, running a rapidly expanding empire," said Joe.

"How long would all this take?" asked the fisherman.

"Not long at all. Maybe 7 to 10 years," replied Joe." With me as your CEO, I'll bet we can do it in 6 years if we hustle. I'm all about the hustle!"

"Wow. Then what?" asked the fisherman.

Joe grinned and said, "Well, here's the best part. When the time is right, we could take the company public or sell the enterprise to the highest bidder. At that point, you would be very rich — a millionaire many times over."

"Really? A millionaire? Then what?" asked the fisherman.

"What do you mean?" asked Joe.

"I mean, what would I do if I was a millionaire?" asked the fisherman.

"Whatever you like," said Joe. "You could retire, move to a tiny coastal village, fish a little, play with your kids ... stroll into the village each night to sip wine ... and play guitar with your wife and friends ... and ..."

49

Without another word, Joe and the fisherman shared a good laugh. As the fisherman wrapped up business, he invited Joe to join him back on the beach later that afternoon. Around sunset, the fisherman had already built a small fire to share his catch of the day with friends. Joe took a seat, tasted the greatest fish he had ever had, and smiled wide. Joe and the fisherman then watched the sun go down as the sound of guitars rose from the village nearby ...

Ahhh, the good life.

Perspective

From Harvard Joe to the island fisherman, success or happiness mean different things to everyone at different stages in life. The only question is how soon we define success, act on our convictions to achieve it, and appreciate others along the way. To that end, here's a little perspective ...

- A **child** dreams of becoming an artist, athlete, or rock 'n' roller.

- **Students** and **professionals** strive for status and financial achievement.

- An **athlete** aspires to break records and win championships.

- **Parents** want health, happiness, and opportunity for their kids.

- In a **third-world village**, success is often defined by access to food, shoes, shelter, education, medicine, and clean water.

- **Volunteers** and **social entrepreneurs** measure success by giving back.

Clearly, definitions vary, but happy people share a common thread. They define success in a manner that inspires them; often tied to their passion and purpose. In the end, success is more than a number. It's a journey without compromise of principles or purpose. At some point, we all have to define it.

Are you there yet?

Final Thoughts

"80% of success is showing up."
Woody Allen (1935 –)
American Actor, Writer, Director

"Find a career you love and you'll never work a day in your life."
Confucius (551 bc – 479 bc)
Chinese Philosopher

It's your life. Strive to do what you love, why you do it, and who you do it with. With these principles in mind, it's time to focus on additional skills for personal and professional success. As you'll discover, each of these skills are not only connected to one another, but to strategies, values, and purpose.

Connect the Dots

How Our Definition of Success Connects to The 4 Essentials	
Skills	» Our definition of success dictates skills we need for growth.
Strategies	» Our definition of success attracts the best teams, mentors, and resources.
Values	» Our definition of success establishes a guiding set of values.
Purpose	» Our definition of success will drive our purpose in life and business.

Exercises and Story Contest

1 Make a list of words that define success for you.
2 From that list, write your definition of success.
3 Write an inspirational story about success.

Rules and Entry Form: www.cliffmichaels.com.

Skill 2
Unleash Your Entrepreneurial Soul

"What's dangerous is not to evolve."
JEFF BEZOS (1964 –)
American Entrepreneur, Founder of Amazon.com

"Being realistic is the most common road to mediocrity."
WILL SMITH (1968 –)
American Actor, Producer, Pop Music Rapper

Set No Limits

From classroom to boardroom and battle field to playing field, we're all entrepreneurs. Be it an artist, athlete, or CEO, we have much to learn from pioneers who boldly go where others only dream. This includes interns at the mail room or baristas in a coffee shop. By definition, entrepreneurs lie awake at night with a driving force that says, "There's a better way." At the core is imagination, a search for innovation, and a mission to improve the human experience.

In my career, I've built companies in real estate, technology, and education. I've also been a speaker and strategist. Like many entrepreneurs, I'm a restless soul. Fortunately, I never feared work and had no illusions about writing a book on *success principles* — a genre that's been covered by many writers with many theories. I knew it would take at least a year. Sure enough, it took four. Finally, after sifting through hundreds of essays written since college, I unleashed a starving part of my entrepreneurial soul — author, Cliff Michaels.

In high school, I always wanted to be a journalist. By college however, I opted for a career in real estate, thinking it was more practical. Then the idea for this book came along. I wondered how I might share my journey and lessons learned. I kept coming back to my favorite strategy – the power of *what if? What if* I broke tradition with old-school success theories? *What if* I wrote a book that ignored format rules, but could help millions of students and professionals? Then it hit me. From party planner to business globetrotter, successful people use the same question quiver to jump-start ideas:

- What if ?
- Why not ?
- When can we start ?
- Who do we know that's been down this road ?
- What worked? What didn't? What lessons were learned ?

The best follow-up question to these "what ifs" and "why nots" is, "What's the best use of my time and effort?" I'm convinced the most successful entrepreneur masters this question so they can **focus on what they do best, then delegate, collaborate, or eliminate the rest.**

Armed with the right questions, every entrepreneur is ready for a personal renaissance. To that end, let's explore a few of my favorite mentors, past and present ...

The Renaissance of Entrepreneurs

Some of my earliest mentors came from history. I think the Renaissance Age was my favorite (14th to 17th centuries). This era conjures up images of new art, cultural change, and boundless imagination. I first studied innovators like Leonardo da Vinci: a painter, inventor, writer, architect, and scientist.

In my literary travels to the 18th century, I discovered Benjamin Franklin: a diplomat, inventor, author, activist, and theorist. I was no less intrigued by the genius of Thomas Edison in the 20th century. With over 1000 patents, Edison invented everything from the phonograph and motion picture camera to stock-tickers and long-lasting light bulbs. More on these mentors later.

Can you imagine what da Vinci, Franklin, and Edison might have done with access to Google? What these innovative giants did more than anything else was throw away conventional thinking. They asked, "What if?" They were dreamers who unleashed entrepreneurial thinking.

Are you ready to unleash ...?

We All Start as Virgins

INNOCENT, CURIOUS, INEXPERIENCED — those are a few words to describe British billionaire, Richard Branson. At least they were until he turned the Virgin moniker into one of the most recognized and successful brands in history. Genius? Advantages? Privileged child? Not exactly. His mother was so determined to make him independent, she stopped the car miles from their house one day and made little Richard find his way home across the fields — as the story goes, he was just 4 and got lost. Dyslexia was an early battle as well, but as Branson says, it likely made him "a better reader of people and situations." Was this perspective the start of something big?

Branson had no business background starting out. To the contrary, he was such a poor academic student, he didn't finish high school. After 40 years of winging it however, Branson's Virgin Group boasts hundreds of companies in 30 countries with over 50,000 employees. This colossal triumph in everything from health and finance to travel and entertainment begs a few questions. What was Branson's competitive advantage and where did this entrepreneurial spirit begin?

Born in London, 1950, Branson started a magazine at 16 with no formal training, merely a desire to make his mark on the world. The publication was called *Student*. The mission was to shake up contemporary thinking in the late '60s. At the same time, there was a culture of activism and new music on the horizon which young Richard embraced.

The experience of running a magazine forced Branson to learn success principles. He once said, "I wanted to be an editor or a journalist. I wasn't really interested in being an entrepreneur, but I soon found I had to become an entrepreneur to keep my magazine going." The magazine only made a few thousand dollars each year, but it was a stepping stone to his Virgin record business, founded in 1972.

> **I suppose Branson is a bit of a kindred spirit for me.**
> **Dyslexic journalist falls ass-backward into entrepreneurship.**

Branson's early record business was fueled by clever use of ad space in the back of *Student* magazine. He then opened a retail record store, built a studio, and started signing recording artists. At the suggestion of an early employee, the corporate name Virgin was proposed because Branson and his peers were new to business. Branson was just 22. A big part of his formula in a highly competitive music industry was taking chances others wouldn't. Specifically, there was a new sound called punk. Branson began signing controversial artists such as

The Sex Pistols. Before anyone realized the changing landscape, Virgin Records was so hot, they signed everyone from Boy George's Culture Club to mega stars like the Rolling Stones and Phil Collins. By the '80s, Virgin became one of the top labels in the world.

Flying high, Branson soon launched Virgin Atlantic Airways, but with business struggling in 1992, he had to sell the record label to keep his airline going. It was a challenging time, but EMI Records acquired Virgin Records for a reported $1 billion dollars. As a result, Branson and Virgin continued to take flight.

By 2010, Branson was as well known for Virgin as he was for daredevil journeys in hot-air balloons. However, it was a creative, down-to-earth business style, with the passion of an adventurist, that connected Branson to customers, employees, and partners alike. People related to Branson because he was genuine. He stripped away the mask of pretentious suits and ties to unleash a unique business artist. The juxtaposition of hippy-like rebel with affable leadership skills made Branson a unique study for virtually anyone interested in unleashing their innovative soul.

In my view, there are many *Essentials* in Branson's toolbox. Chief among them is an uncanny ability to infuse entrepreneurial spirit within his corporate cultures. After all, Branson doesn't run 200 companies himself. What he does extraordinarily well is empower others to unleash their inner CEO; including new employees and senior executives alike. In that regard, Branson is known more for his bottom-up managerial style than a top-down regime. He challenges others to think creatively. He encourages teams to work with passion and gives them an environment to develop talent. "Let's have fun and provide extraordinary customer experience," is as much the Branson mantra as "Let's make money."

Branson plays to his strongest *Essentials*. His key **skills** include passion, imagination, and perseverance. Focus **strategies** include communication and democratic leadership. Core **values** include integrity, humility, and commitment. No less important are Branson's **purpose** principles; a life centered on family, adventure, and making a difference in the world.

In short, Branson is a master of entrepreneurial thinking. He doesn't just talk about mission, vision, and values. He lives them. Through his philanthropic arm, Virgin Unite, his humanitarian efforts include protecting human rights, preserving the environment, and supporting education. He's worked with world leaders from Nelson Mandela to activists such as Peter Gabriel. He was even knighted for his contributions to a generation of entrepreneurs (Sir Richard, if you please).

Growing up, I had no idea who Richard Branson was. Early in my career, I was even less interested in studying billionaires because I found them unapproachable. Their stories of privilege didn't always connect with most people. Then the Branson principles found their way into my research. Kind of hard to miss. Fact is, most of us will never run 200 companies or reach billionaire status — nice work if you can get it. Many of us just want to create exceptional art, build a small business, be great at what we do, or enjoy a simple life. Branson shows us that nothing is impossible if ambition is connected to *4 Essentials*.

Remember, we all start as virgins. So when you get your next big idea, don't ask "Why?" Think like Branson and ask, "Why not?"

See Your Future

There are multitalented people who see the future, set no limits, then unleash their entrepreneurial soul. Among them are fast-growth brands like Tony Hawk (skateboard champion and video-game juggernaut), Oprah Winfrey (producer, publisher, talk-show host), and cross-over entertainers like Jay-Z, Beyonce, Will Smith, and Jennifer Lopez (TV, music, film, fashion). Other pioneers with a *single-company focus* include Sergey Brin and Larry Page (Google), Howard Schultz (Starbucks), Bill Gates (Microsoft), Steve Jobs (Apple), Jeff Bezos (Amazon), and Mark Zuckerberg (Facebook). However, it might be interesting to analyze talent beyond the usual suspects, so let's shake up our paradigm a bit. What's an entrepreneur ... *really?*

When I look at my mentors, one lady taught me as much as anyone else when it comes to vision and creating something that stands the test of time. If you watched any television in the past fifty years, you couldn't have missed *I Love Lucy* (1951-1957), the comedic brainchild of Lucille Ball and Desi Arnaz. It was the longest-running syndicated show in television history (still is, last I checked). But do you know the full entrepreneurial story behind the goofy redhead and stylish, Cuban bandleader?

Lucille Ball was initially told by drama school teachers she had no future in entertainment (cue live-audience laugh track). From the 1930s to the 1970s, Lucy was a model, dancer, singer, radio voice, theater performer, film and television actress. Oh, and arguably the greatest female comedian in history. She had one of the longest careers in Hollywood and was the first woman to head a major studio. Husband, Desi Arnaz (Ricky Ricardo), was a talented actor, singer, and business maverick in his own right.

Together, Lucy and Desi not only had the foresight to create their own production company, Desilu Studios, they retained ownership and distribution

57

rights of their intellectual property, including *I Love Lucy*. Another layer to the Lucy-Desi genius was the use of multiple camera angles and motion-picture film quality in front of a live, studio audience. Lucy and Desi understood that traditional TV standards back in the '50s wouldn't stand the test of time. To recoup high production costs, they needed quality reruns that would have future demand. Many forget that Desilu was home to some of the most valued shows in TV history such as *Star Trek, Mission Impossible, The Untouchables, The Andy Griffith Show,* and *The Dick Van Dyke Show*. These franchises thrived for decades, long after they were created.

While Desi was half the genius behind Desilu, it was Lucy who broke new ground in a male-dominated profession at a time when it was neither fashionable or politically correct to do so. She also broke the glass ceiling for a generation of entertainers to see themselves as business owners, not merely performers. Just look at the talented comedian-entrepreneurs who followed in Lucy's footsteps from Carol Burnett in the '70s to modern moguls like Tina Fey and Ellen DeGeneres. Lucy and Desi also set the stage for modern Hollywood power couples, not to mention millions of entrepreneurs who learned the value of seeing their future, then packaging a product or image to ensure the test of time.

This short essay is just my way of saying, "Thanks" to Lucy and Desi for future-proofing a ton of laughs and unleashing a unique set of entrepreneurial lessons.

Be Fearless

In my view, anyone with courage and unique ability is an entrepreneur. Therefore, this book wouldn't be complete without honoring my favorite, groundbreaking athletes, Muhammad Ali and Jackie Robinson.

After winning a Gold medal in the 1960 Olympics, and becoming Heavyweight Champion of the world, Ali was in the prime of his career. Tragically, he was stripped of his World Heavyweight Title in 1967 (age 25) due to his protest of the Vietnam War. He had also changed his name from Cassius Clay to Muhammad Ali to proudly stand on his principles as a Muslim. It's sad to think that fifty years later we still have fear mongers and political fanatics believing Muslims by definition are terrorists; but that's a point I'll reserve for the tolerance chapter later in this book. Imagine the persecution Ali faced at a time when civil activism was just catching on in the late '60s. Here are a few words that capture Ali's views back in the day:

*"I ain't got no quarrel with the Viet Cong ... I'm not going
10,000 miles to help murder, burn, and drop bombs on brown
people in Vietnam while so-called Negro people in Louisville
are treated like dogs and denied simple, human rights."*

Ali's protest placed him center stage of the civil rights movement. Refusing to be drafted, he faced up to five years in prison. At the same time, the New York State Athletic Commission stripped Ali of his boxing license.

Public support was mixed but a groundswell of Americans supported Ali. While his case was up for appeal, the Supreme Court ruled that the Athletic Commission had unjustly stripped Ali of his boxing license. Then in March 1971, Ali regained the Heavyweight Title from an undefeated Joe Frazier. Three months later, the Supreme Court reversed the charges against Ali. Poetic justice served, Ali became one of the most beloved sports figures, a 3-Time World Champion, and a global peacemaker.

Then there was Jackie Robinson, breaking ground twenty years before Ali. Born into poverty in Cairo, Georgia (1919), Jackie was the first athlete at UCLA to letter in four varsity sports (track, football, baseball, basketball). An excellent student, only financial hardship prohibited Jackie from getting his college degree. He considered it a small setback and decided to pursue a football career in Honolulu. Unfortunately, he was drafted to fight in World War II, halting his football career. Commissioned as a second lieutenant, Jackie's military career was then interrupted when he refused to go to the back of a segregated bus in 1944. Jackie consequently faced a court martial on the bus charges but was acquitted (ironically by an all-white jury). Honorably discharged from the military, Jackie had to start his career over — again.

An athlete at heart, Jackie joined the Kansas City Monarchs baseball club of the Negro Leagues in 1945. He was soon spotted by Brooklyn Dodgers' executive, Branch Rickey. Rickey offered Jackie the opportunity to sign with the Dodgers' international farm club, the Montreal Royals. What were the *Essential* qualifiers? Rickey signed Jackie not only for his athletic talent, but he saw in Jackie a man of exceptional character. Breaking the color barrier would require a player of tremendous focus and courage; a man who could turn the other cheek in the face of certain ridicule, even death threats, as Major League Baseball's first African American player. The rest is stuff legends are made of — Jackie was Rookie of the Year when he turned pro in 1947. He was National League MVP in 1949 and helped the Brooklyn Dodgers win their first World Championship in 1955 against arch rivals, the New York Yankees.

Considering athletes today, often spoiled by a sense of entitlement, the humanitarian contributions of Ali and Robinson should play a role in sports education. Like my soccer idol Pelé, Ali and Robinson are legends to be revered for centuries, not solely for athletic achievement — they are beloved human beings because they unleashed fearless, entrepreneurial souls.

We're All Entrepreneurs

"Create fun and a little weirdness — be adventurous and open-minded."
Tony Hsieh (1973 –)
American Entrepreneur, CEO, Zappos.com, Author - *Delivering Happiness*

I've touched on a few pioneers who influenced my life. We could just as easily talk about courageous leaders like Gandhi and Mandela, breakthrough scientists like Einstein and Galileo, or music legends like Aretha Franklin and The Beatles. Bottom line ... it's cool to be different. Rock the boat a little!

These days, entrepreneurs come in all shapes and sizes; from artists and bloggers to chefs and singers. It's the violinist with a funky hat. It's the 10-year-old with a lemonade stand. It's the street dancer who blends ballet and break dancing. It's the doctor who listens before pontificating. It's grandma with her super-tasty, gluten-free, dairy-free, vegan-cookie recipes!

If you get the gist of this chapter, we're all entrepreneurs.
The question is, "Which one are you?"

Final Thoughts

"To become indispensable involves doing difficult work ...
engaging in tasks that require maturity, soul, and personal strength.
The hard work is being brave enough to make a difference."
SETH GODIN (1960 –)
American Entrepreneur, Author

ONE OF MY FAVORITE bloggers is author, Seth Godin, famous for advise on social marketing. A recurring theme in one of his books, *Linchpin*, is that no matter what we do in life, each of us is an artist — the more in touch we are with our inner artisan, the more indispensable we are as employees or business owners. Similar to Seth's analogy, I encourage friends in all walks of life to unleash their entrepreneurial soul.

So whether you're a CEO, Snowboard Sensei, or International Girl of Mystery, be sure to fall in love with the entrepreneur's credo, "What if?" For naysayers who question your utter lack of common sense, simply reply, "Why not?"

Connect the Dots

How The Entrepreneurial Soul Connects to The 4 Essentials	
SKILLS	» Entrepreneurial thinking builds creativity and commitment. In turn, skills and experience are accelerated.
STRATEGIES	» Entrepreneurial thinking improves teamwork, leadership, problem solving, and self-discovery.
VALUES	» Entrepreneurial thinking ignites a search for truth. This search develops integrity, humility, patience, and gratitude.
PURPOSE	» Entrepreneurial thinking inspires courage, resolve, and a sense of adventure in ourselves and those around us.

Exercises and Story Contest

1 List your top 3 strengths as an entrepreneur.
2 Write an inspirational story about the entrepreneurial soul.

RULES AND ENTRY FORM: www.cliffmichaels.com.

Skill 3
Build a Passion for Learning

> *"Study without desire spoils the memory,*
> *and it retains nothing that it takes in."*
> LEONARDO DA VINCI (1452 – 1519)
> Italian Painter, Scientist, Inventor

The Big Secret Is ...

Who are we kidding? There are no secrets; just *Essential* reminders. If there were a magic elixir, we'd all be super healthy, crazy wealthy, and insanely happy. Having said that, there's one *Essential* none of us can do without — a thirst for knowledge. This includes a genuine curiosity about ourselves and others. Who am I? What drives her? Who's on my team and what's their appetite for knowledge?

Simply stated, when we learn and share, we grow.

Heart of The Oprah Effect

BORN INTO POVERTY AND a childhood filled with hardship, Oprah Winfrey's journey is one of the more intriguing stories in modern history. With the highest-rated talk show on television, she became not only the world's first African-American, female billionaire, but one of the most influential people on the planet. If anyone wants to discover the *Essential* arrow in Oprah's success quiver, look no further than her passion for learning.

At a time when book sales were on the decline and dumbed-down talk shows were on the rise, Oprah did something unheard of. She launched *Oprah's Book Club* in 1996, making it socially cool for millions of viewers to discuss literature. From classics to pop culture, Oprah's influence became so relevant that if she introduced a book it became a bestseller. This marketing bonanza became synonymous with *The Oprah Effect.*

So where did it all start for the talk-show diva? In spite of a childhood that began with poverty and abuse, Oprah says she was blessed to have a grandmother who taught her to read at age three. She ended up skipping two early grades and became an honor student. After winning an oratory contest, she earned a full scholarship to Tennessee State University where she studied communication. She then worked at a local radio station during early college years and became the youngest female news anchor at Nashville's WLAC-TV. By 1983, she landed a gig hosting *AM Chicago*, a poorly-rated TV talk show before Oprah arrived. Oprah catapulted the show from last place to #1 in America, surpassing Phil Donahue, a pioneer in the talk-show genre. How did Oprah do it?

Oprah had a unique sense of what made people tick. Her communication style connected on a visceral level, especially with a female audience. She also understood the power of social media long before Facebook and Twitter were in vogue. Moreover, her passion for reading, giving, and self-discovery raised the bar for personal growth, not just television ratings. In short, she had a social experience worth sharing.

In the big scheme, no one can argue with Oprah's results. During her unprecedented talk-show run of 25 years, she launched *Oprah.com*, *O Magazine*, and the *Oprah Winfrey Network. TIME Magazine* included Oprah on their list of "100 Most Influential People of the 20th Century." Through *Oprah's Angel Network*, she has raised millions of dollars for charities worldwide. Oprah even created a Leadership Academy in South Africa to provide education and opportunity for underprivileged girls.

Did all this stem from privilege? Hardly. It was a focus on reading, education, and a passion for the human condition. These *Essentials* were Oprah's path to not only living her best life, but encouraging millions to do the same.

Know Your Best Learning Style

Growing up, I didn't realize I had a semi-dyslexic challenge with math and reading. For starters, I hated numbers unless they were on a sports page. It's a bit ironic I went into real estate — thank goodness for calculators. Computers were the ultimate mind-screw for me too. I loved reading and writing but comprehension was no picnic — I usually had to read a page several times to get it. It took daily practice for about ten years before I mastered a few speed-reading skills in my late teens. Writing letters each day helped a lot. Adding to the fun, my right brain (creative guy) likes to battle my left brain (organization dude). Between the left-brain, right-brain, semi-dyslexia, and attention-deficit thing, it's quite a party!

Finally, around 30, a friend clued me in about our unique learning styles. He was a shy musician but very in tune with others. He was also a smart entrepreneur who built successful companies by surrounding himself with talented people who made up for his business shortcomings. He pointed out that I was highly verbal, visual, and social, but weak in math and logical thinking. At the time, I thought I could read people well, but he had me pegged. I soon appreciated that if each of us could recognize our best learning style, and the unique style of others, it would be easier to focus on strengths and shore up weaknesses (fill our gaps).

Here's what I discovered next as many parents and educators know all too well. Some people learn best through listening, discussion, and self-reflection. Examples include philosophers, psychologists, and counselors. Others learn best through social interaction, such as politicians, networkers, or salespeople. Some are more verbal and comfortable with words, like writers, lawyers, and journalists. Painters, designers, and photographers learn best through visual means. There are those who analyze the world through logic and math such as scientists, engineers, and economists. Kinesthetic folks such as athletes, dancers, and yogis develop insight through touch and physical movement. Let's not forget those in tune to music, rhythm, or sound such as singers, musicians, and composers. We even have a category for environmentalists — the ones who connect with their surroundings. In short, we all have unique abilities. Some are stronger by nature. Others must be nurtured.

Conceived in 1983, early credit in the study of different learning abilities goes to Harvard psychology professor, Dr. Howard Gardner. In his book, *Frames of Mind: The Theory of Multiple Intelligences,* Gardner suggested that traditional theories measuring intelligence are too limiting, such as I.Q. testing. He therefore proposed a more modern idea known as multiple intelligences.

Similar theories are well illustrated in two of my favorite books, *Emotional Intelligence* and *Social Intelligence*, both by another Harvard psychology professor, Dr. Daniel Goleman. What always served me best from these psychology lessons was a blueprint to reading people and situations. I'll leave the neurology chat to my esteemed peers with Ph.Ds, but when it comes to life skills, I think these core essentials are the most indispensable.

1 **Emotional Intelligence:** Our self-awareness, self-discipline, and ability to manage emotions. This is a basic understanding of *what drives me*.

2 **Social Intelligence:** Our ability to empathize, get along, and read situations. This is a basic understanding of *what drives other people*.

These skills not only provide insight to how we learn, they illustrate how strength or weakness in one ability can dramatically affect another. In the case of our *4 Essentials*, what good are skills without action strategies, self-awareness without social abilities, or abilities without values and purpose?

Intelligence Type		Definition
EMOTIONAL	»	Self-aware, self-reflective
SOCIAL	»	Empathetic, strong people skills
VERBAL	»	Effective with spoken or written words
VISUAL	»	Spatial awareness of views, pictures, objects
LOGICAL, MATHEMATICAL	»	Intuitive with numbers, patterns, reasoning
KINESTHETIC, TACTILE	»	In touch with body, movement, athletics
MUSICAL	»	In tune with sound, tones, rhythms
NATURALISTIC	»	In touch with nature and surroundings

With so many different learning styles, there's no need to be frustrated if we don't master them all. No one does. The key is humility. We simply have to ask, "Where can I improve? Is there a person or tool that bridges a gap between what I don't know, don't do well, don't have time for, or don't like to do?"

If we approach life and business with these simple questions, no one is limited to their innate abilities or intelligence. A world-class athlete may not be a software wiz, but he can add a computer buddy to his network. An introverted doctor with lousy people skills can learn to be more empathetic by hiring a friendly staff. A shy entrepreneur would do well to partner with socially savvy salespeople. Peer-to-peer learning is also one of the most dymanic ways to **M**aster **B**asic **A**bilities.

In many ways, we're only limited by the company we keep or who we study. If we become more self-aware and socially friendly, it's much easier to select compatible friends, employees, or partners. With a little luck or practice, peer intelligence might even rub off, not merely fill our gaps.

Final Thoughts

"An investment in knowledge always pays the best interest."
BENJAMIN FRANKLIN (1706 – 1790)
American Politician, Author, Inventor

THE SOONER WE FOCUS on strongest abilities, including our best learning style, the sooner we can leverage someone else's skills or intelligence. We'll discuss more of these strategies, such as tools and mentors, in the next chapter, but as we continue to explore entrepreneurial thinking, always come back to this principle:

The relentless pursuit of knowledge, especially about ourselves and others, is critical to personal and professional growth.

Connect the Dots

How My Passion for Learning Connects to The 4 Essentials	
SKILLS	» Knowledge is essential to building peak-performance abilities.
STRATEGIES	» Knowledge facilitates teamwork, leadership, communication, problem solving, and project planning.
VALUES	» The acquisition of knowledge requires humility and patience.
PURPOSE	» The sooner we have knowledge, the sooner we can apply it.

Exercises and Story Contest

1 List your top 3 intelligence types and 3 favorite learning styles.
2 Write a story about a knowledge quest that resulted in success.

RULES AND ENTRY FORM: www.cliffmichaels.com.

Skill 4
Leverage Tools and Mentors

"If I have seen further,
it is by standing on the shoulders of giants."
SIR ISAAC NEWTON (1642 – 1727)
English Physicist, Mathematician, Philosopher

Part 1: The Martial Art of Leverage

I COULDN'T WRITE THIS chapter without honoring another one of my child-hood idols, martial arts master, Bruce Lee (1940-1973). I began studying Lee's principles when I was about 13, mostly through his films and a few books about his life. By the time I was in my early 20s, Lee's genius became even more relevant as I engaged in real-world battles.

Widely recognized as the pioneer of mixed martial arts, Lee broke tradition with rigid fighting tenets by developing his own combat style called *Jeet Kune Do: The Way of the Intercepting Fist*. At its core, *Jeet Kune Do* embraced many forms and weapons. As a result, Lee could easily flow from one adversary to another. He was as fluid in American boxing as he was in Chinese kung fu. He was as swift with sticks as he was nimble with nunchucks.

For me, Lee's philosophy translates well into life and the workplace. We're all warriors, seeking tools and mentors that can save time, money, or effort. Fortunately, essential resources are simpler than ever to leverage. We can research information online. We can engage social and business networks across the globe with the click of a mouse. We can even study a foreign language while jogging. The Edisons and Einsteins of the world never had it so good.

At the end of the day, there's little benefit to being a **Chief Everything Officer**. I was guilty of this in my 20s, running my business as the sales leader, company captain, and operations guy. Finally, I wised up. I stopped doing things I wasn't good at, didn't know, didn't like to do, or didn't have time for. I fell in love with leverage — delegating, collaborating, and eliminating.

Risks of Leverage

I would do everyone a disservice if I didn't also point out the shortcomings of leverage. Trying to delegate or outsource every life or business task isn't as simple as ordering take-out pizza. There's a risk of time, money, and effort each time we add new partners or hire experts. Trust and talent aren't a sure bet just because someone's résumé says so. Personality conflicts and work ethics don't necessarily show up in interviews. How about the learning curve of new systems or time and cost to train new people? Truth is, even with references, we'll never know until we try. However, we can minimize risk and maximize leverage every time.

We simply have to ask, "Who's been down this road before ...?"

Part 2: Many Tasks, Many Mentors

We all have our favorite mentor and each has something to offer (coach, author, teacher, business brain, talk-show host). Having said that, the idea of just one mentor makes absolutely no sense. No single person can teach us everything in life or business. The smartest peers or public pontificators may be experts in one field but amateurs in another. We also carry the bias and baggage of mentors as well as their wisdom.

The secret is to learn best practices from those who have been there, done that, and preferably *done that exceptionally well*. Regardless, not all advice will prove wise or reliable. Moreover, just because someone has material success, it doesn't make them a happy or successful human being. From friends and family to iconic billionaires, some are wonderful people worth emulating. Others are not. The key is surrounding ourselves with people who have talent, integrity, and experience.

And then ...?

Listen and Learn

Some of the people who influenced the earliest years of my life rarely listened and tended to interrupt, including my parents (bless their hearts). Consequently, one of my weakest skills is listening. I think most of us can improve in this area, especially the over-zealous entrepreneur. We sometimes struggle with our passion to speak when it's often wise to listen and learn. The cardinal rule — one mouth, two ears — use them in that proportion. That was a tough for me to learn as a highly verbal person. (Bare with me, I'm still working on it). However, some mentors vastly improved my listening skills. My gratitude is overdue ...

Meet My Virtual Mentor, Charlie

When friends ask about my favorite mentors, I often point to someone I've never met; a man with a far more voracious appetite for knowledge than my own, Mr. Charlie Rose. He's been the host and producer of *The Charlie Rose Show* since 1991. An Emmy-winning, broadcast journalist, Charlie engages the world's most fascinating thinkers and news makers in one-on-one roundtable interviews.

Famous for his no-frills oak table, pitch-black studio background, and commercial-free hour format, dropping in on a Charlie Rose conversation is like an evening ticket to a think-tank. In a week, viewers can pick up best practices from business leaders like Jeff Bezos at Amazon, literary advice from novelists such as John Grisham, or philanthropy insight from Bill Gates and Warren Buffett.

A month at Charlie's roundtable also provides political opinions from world leaders, respected views from the finest journalists, and breakthrough ideas from pioneers in science and medicine. Charlie even mixes it up with stars from the arts, sports, and entertainment world. You're as likely to see Jay-Z or Steven Spielberg as you are Lance Armstrong or Angelina Jolie.

Equally important is the mutual respect, civil discourse, and intelligent banter Rose engenders. Listening intently is as much his gift as challenging views. In a media era that encourages shouting rather than talking, drama over substance, and commercial interruptions by the minute, Rose breaks all the rules. He's a perfect example of a mentor you may never meet, but can learn from every night.

Rose's show is accessible to anyone with cable TV or Internet access. So if you haven't found your favorite guru, drop in on my virtual mentor, Charlie. Then kick back and let the intelligence sink in.

My Other Favorite Mentor – TED

Another great source for mentors are TED Talks devoted to *Ideas Worth Spreading.* By 2011, TED Talks had been viewed online by millions. It all started as a conference in 1984, merging three worlds: Technology - Entertainment - Design. TED's scope has broadened since; including artists and thinkers from all walks of life. Each speaker is given up to 18 minutes for presentations. You're as likely to hear breakthrough ideas from illusionists and street dancers as you are Bill Clinton or Malcolm Gladwell.

TED's curator is a former British journalist and publisher, Chris Anderson. Under his stewardship, Anderson has revolutionized web-based learning. TEDx events are now worldwide, but you can always view TED Talks free online.

Choosing Mentors

When selecting mentors, look for people you not only respect, but who've reached a level of success (especially happiness) you aspire to. You'll want mentors with teaching methods that fit your style. If you're visual, you may not click with someone who's strictly verbal. If you're logical, someone who doesn't explain how things work may drive you nuts. If you're lazy, you may need a drill sergeant!

Some life coaches know little about business and many business coaches have no idea what it takes to live a balanced life. The "experts" have flaws like all of us. Don't build them up to be something they're not. Ultimately, we want mentors who challenge us and share a common passion. Regardless of who you work with, always ask three questions:

1) What worked? **2)** What didn't work? **3)** What lessons were learned?

Once we get those knowledge nuggets, our path is unlimited.

Mirror the Masters

To be the best, study extraordinary people. Writers? Twain influenced me as much as Dickens and Salinger. Art? Too many to list but Picasso was certainly out of the box! Music? I learned as much from Stevie Wonder and The Beatles as I did from Mozart. Movies? Spielberg, Scorsese, and Hitchcock directed my appreciation for film. Science? Einstein and Hawking taught me things about the universe I never imagined. Investments? Warren Buffett makes no secret about his money strategies. Is comedy your shtick? My favorite goofballs are Lucille Ball, Jon Stewart, George Carlin, and the Saturday Night Live cast through the years.

Study one. Study them all. Mirror the Masters.

Final Thoughts

"Teachers open the door. You enter by yourself."
CHINESE PROVERB

IN ADDITION TO SEEKING mentors, there's great satisfaction in being one. Mentoring a student or young professional is a surefire method to fine-tune skills while helping others. The more we develop talented people in harmony with our *4 Essentials*, the more we can delegate or collaborate. The more we can leverage, the more time we have for fun, friends, family, and new ventures.

Connect the Dots

How Leverage Connects to The 4 Essentials	
SKILLS	» Tools and mentors accelerate the learning curve.
STRATEGIES	» Leverage supports teamwork and time management.
VALUES	» Leverage requires humility and gratitude.
PURPOSE	» Leverage saves time, money, and effort.

Exercises and Story Contest

1 List your top 3 tools or mentors that make your life easier.
2 Write a story on tools or mentors that improved your life or business.

RULES AND ENTRY FORM: www.cliffmichaels.com.

Skill 5
Cultivate Curiosity and Creativity

> *"There are two ways of being creative.*
> *One can sing and dance ... or one can create an environment*
> *where singers and dancers can flourish."*
> WARREN BENNIS (1925 –)
> American Scholar, Author, Leadership Consultant

Unlock Your Inner Da Vinci

A FEW YEARS AFTER college, I was sitting in a cafe, listening to friends chat about Leonardo da Vinci. My pals were artists and engineers so I was the odd man out as a real estate broker. They went on for hours about how to learn from the genius of da Vinci, the renaissance archetype (scientist, engineer, painter, sculptor, inventor). "How do you study genius?" I asked. "Are any of us likely to paint the *Mona Lisa* merely by studying da Vinci's paintings? They looked upon me as a silly child not paying attention. "Cliff, you study successful people and you never studied da Vinci?" Right then, I knew I was in for a lesson.

As my friends explained, da Vinci had a system that nourished curiosity and fostered passions for work, play, and learning. His principles have been widely chronicled and practiced by individuals and corporations for centuries. Although often known as a man of mystery, (eloquently, if not fictionally dramatized by Dan Brown's blockbuster novel, *The Da Vinci Code*), da Vinci recorded thousands of pages in personal notebooks that provide insight to his process for innovation. In fact, da Vinci's system for cultivating curiosity and creativity was based on connectedness; the primary tenet of *The 4 Essentials*.

Published around 1684, 165 years after his death, da Vinci's journals reveal that he scribbled notes and drawings every day, on virtually everything. From inventions to philosophy, and sketches to diagrams, he had a system of *connecting* everything he saw. He synthesized science and art, medicine and music, culture and new ideas. Many have said that his notes were so random they lacked order, but that was his genius — da Vinci could go from subject to subject in the blink of an eye. Ironically, da Vinci was considered attention deficit by some historians, maybe dyslexic. He failed to finish many things he started. Perhaps his greatest genius was the use of apprentices and journal systems to compensate for occasional focus failure — just a crazy theory I have.

Yes, da Vinci had something many of us aren't born with; an extraordinary curiosity and creative intelligence. However, contrary to popular belief, curiosity and creativity are skills that can be acquired. From what we know of da Vinci, his **M**astery of **B**asic **A**bilities always started with plenty of *what ifs* and *why nots?* Most of us can do that. From there, his success was driven as much by creative routines as any born-genius. Simply stated, da Vinci was a master of journals, discussion, and experimentation (roots of entrepreneurial thinking).

As a fascinating footnote to history, Microsoft founder, Bill Gates, paid a reported $30 million dollars for one of the da Vinci notebooks, *The Codex Leicester*. If studying the notes of da Vinci was good enough for Gates, maybe there's a lesson here. As Einstein said, "Success is not about what you can memorize."

So let's summarize the da Vinci code to unlock your creative genius:

CREATIVE STEP 1: DISCUSS AND EXPERIMENT
Talk about ideas. Then put words into action.

CREATIVE STEP 2: BE CURIOUS AND PASSIONATE
Maintain an insatiable passion about people, places, and things.

CREATIVE STEP 3: SURROUND YOURSELF WITH TALENT
Cultivate friends, teams, and coworkers who think outside the box. Creativity will rise to the level of your peers.

CREATIVE STEP 4: MAINTAIN A PRIVATE JOURNAL OR PUBLIC BLOG
Whatever you see, think, or hear each day, write it down. From ideas and humor to health and relationships, set no limits.

P.S. I'm No Genius

As confessed, math and science always kicked my ass. I failed everything from high school chemistry to college calculus. I've always struggled with computers. I did however crack the da Vinci code as a freshman at USC. Since my memory skills were nothing to brag about, I always carried a pen and notepad to scribble ideas. If I met you, I jotted down what we talked about. I also kept a journal next to my bed. I still do. These days, I e-mail myself a good idea from my cell phone; genius recall thanks to modern technology.

Conclusion: *If da Vinci teaches us nothing else, it's that genius is as much about routines as any talent we're born with. Wanna think like da Vinci? Scribble more!*

P.P.S. Take 20% Time-Off

While we're on the subject of genius thinking, let's fast-forward to present day. Most of us know Google as the little engine that not only could, but did. They did it bigger and faster than Yahoo or any search engine before them. Have you ever wondered where all the innovation comes from? Is it the genius of co-founders Larry Page and Sergey Brin who were tinkering with Internet search as Stanford students in 1996? Is it the collective brainpower of 20,000 employees? Experts agree that a big part of the entrepreneurial sparkplug is what Google calls *innovation time*, the 20% rule for cultivating ideas.

By now, business junkies know the lesson and many have adopted the practice. To stimulate innovation and motivate employees, Google workers are encouraged to spend 20% of their week on new ideas that interest them. It could be the next killer application or something more efficient for business development. Some of Google's most widely-used products, such as Gmail and Google News, were born from this practice. Google has even estimated that as much as 50% of their new product launches originate from innovation time, one way or another,

The idea for implementing the 20% Rule at Google goes not only to the vision of Brin and Page, but the stewardship of CEO, Eric Schmidt, a former board member at Apple. Schmidt was brought on to accelerate growth and provide some "parental supervision," as Sergey once said.

Schmidt is often credited with pioneering a 70/20/10 management model that believes innovation is cultivated best when employees spend 70% of their time on core business tasks, 20% on related projects, and 10% on unrelated projects. At some universities, a similar philosophy believes that 70% of learning comes from on-the-job experience, 20% from ongoing work with mentors, and 10% from formal training. Given its meteoric rise to the top of the business food chain, the 20% Rule at Google is clearly a sound strategy.

As a side note to aspiring writers, I was running several companies when I wrote this book. I was always crunched for creative-thinking time. However, when I dedicated just 30 minutes a day to scribbling ideas, the strategies for connecting my essays on success principles started flowing like crazy. My 20% innovation time soon turned into a few hours at night, then one day per week. Passion took over, and I found creative ways to delegate or collaborate editing tasks. I went 20% loco! The result? The book you're now reading.

Carving out innovation time may be tough with daily chaos, but it's worth it. If necessary, unplug the TV or shut off your cell phone. If you need a creative jolt, read a new book or discuss your craziest ideas with friends.

Whatever you do, break routines and get your innovative groove on — you just might become 20% happier and 20% more successful!

Final Thoughts

"Neither a lofty degree of intelligence, nor imagination, nor both together, go to the making of genius. Love, love, love. That is the soul of genius."
WOLFGANG AMADEUS MOZART (1756 – 1791)
German Classical Composer

IT'S NO SECRET THAT da Vinci shared common threads with Mozart, Einstein, and Edison. Besides an innate curiosity and passion for life, each of these geniuses was ridiculed in public. Most notably, Einstein and Edison were considered substandard students. As one story goes, a professor told Einstein he would never amount to anything because he didn't want to learn Greek.

Speaking of learning challenges, the list of other famous people reported to have a form of dyslexia include Magic Johnson, John Lennon, Harrison Ford, Tom Cruise, Charles Schwab, Agatha Christie, and Walt Disney.

So for anyone who ever felt out of place because the world was going too fast or too slow, your creative genius may simply be misunderstood — especially by others who are in fact going too fast or too slow.

Connect The Dots

How Creativity Connects to The 4 Essentials	
SKILLS	» Creativity is essential to entrepreneurial thinking.
STRATEGIES	» Creativity improves decision making and problem solving.
VALUES	» Creativity requires patience, humility, and persistence.
PURPOSE	» Creative people are more playful, adventurous, and solution-oriented.

Exercises and Story Contest

1 List your top 3 creative strategies in life or business.
2 Write an inspirational story on creativity or innovation.

RULES AND ENTRY FORM: www.cliffmichaels.com.

Skill 6
Practice with Passion and Purpose

> *"By nature, men are nearly alike ...*
> *by practice, they get to be wide apart."*
> CONFUCIUS (551 BC – 479 BC)
> Chinese Philosopher

> **Insanity**
> *"Doing the same thing over & over; expecting different results."*
> ALBERT EINSTEIN (1879 – 1955)
> German-Swiss Theoretical Physicist

In Search of Excellence?

I ONCE THOUGHT PRACTICE made perfect. It wasn't until I took up golf in my 20s that I realized how silly that cliché was. No matter how hard Sunday hackers practice that insane slice, they still end up in the woods. Many golfers even get worse with time. Disturbingly worse. So the question isn't whether we practice. It's whether we practice with passion and purpose — is our daily routine result-oriented or just passing time?

In his best-selling book, *Outliers*, Malcolm Gladwell provides insightful stories which reinforce a basic theory; that focus, opportunity, and deliberate practice are critical to success. Gladwell's stories also suggest that being really great at something, such as math, sports, or music, usually requires upwards of 10 years or 10,000 hours of practice. Are these the common threads of Tiger Woods and Wolfgang Mozart, or Bill Gates and Steve Jobs? How about Plain Jane and Average Joe? Do we need special gifts at birth or can each of us achieve extraordinary success through Mastery of Basic Abilities?

Let's explore the myth of born-genius and reality of practice ...

Myth vs. Reality

Each of us has innate skills (kinesthetic athletes, musical composers, logical engineers). Supportive parents obviously play a key role in early development. However, natural gifts and rich environments are not a proxy for success. There are plenty of wayward geniuses who accomplish little. Therefore, the questions we have to ask are: What are the true success formulas in life *and* business, regardless of genes or opportunity? What enabled Mozart, Woods, Gates, or Jobs to reach *prodigy or genius* status, assuming we're anointing anyone with such titles? Do these ultra-talented kids get in line twice for gifts at birth, or do they *master basic abilities* at a very early age through extremely hard work? Upon close inspection, we discover that *genius* is at least dependent upon passion, practice, and purpose as much as any lucky draw of the gene pool.

First, let's look at a few principles we can all relate to — show up, lather, rinse, repeat — pure repetition is how many people practice their life routine Some improve, often they don't (hello fellow golf hackers). Therefore, the tenet *"practice makes perfect"* is fine in theory, but very misguided. People can practice the same craft 20 years and perform no better in year 21 than day 1. If routines have no built-in mechanism for learning (passion and purpose), poor practice will not self-correct.

Now let's examine the outliers, starting with Mozart and Woods. Little Wolfie and Tiger had hyper-focused parents in Leopold Mozart and Earl Woods. Each father had a passion in music composition and golf respectively. Each created an early opportunity for his kid to grow into a skill that the father first mastered to a high degree. Both parents decided in advance their kids were special at birth; let's just say a bit more than the average, loving parent. Next, they mapped a course for greatness and began training their *prodigies* in a single discipline. In other words, Wolfie and Tiger weren't born geniuses (in my opinion). They received expert, around-the-clock instruction, under the watchful eye of emotionally-vested fathers (some say obsessed). Hardly normal circumstances. It's not to say the kids didn't have natural talent. They did. But were they born geniuses?

Wolfgang's father was a public composer, teacher, and disciplinarian. He began teaching piano to young Wolfie at age 3. Historians tell us Leopold had Wolfie composing by 5, and performing publicly at 8. However, there are no composition records in pre-school Wolfie's handwriting, suggesting early composition may have been corrected or written, at least in part, by his father. Wolfie's earliest music as a schoolboy is also said to sound oddly familiar to his contemporaries, particularly those he studied with (*Funny, that's precisely how many recording artists score a good hit; by sampling someone else's work*). This doesn't minimize the greatness of Mozart's music, nor does it imply Mozart lifted a few good tunes, but the notion that he began composing masterpieces out of whole cloth as a gifted preschooler, or from a divine spark, is certainly worth debating.

According to many classical experts, Mozart's greatest achievements occurred between ages 21 and 35. This means little Wolfie's *genius* didn't hit stride until after he hyper-focused 18 to 32 years. This is blasphemy to Mozart lovers who buy the genius-at-birth theory, but fascinating if we're having an honest dialogue about whether a genius is born or developed.

In the athletic world, Tiger Woods is considered a naturally-gifted golf genius. In reality, it's the Mozart story on the links. Not dissimilar to Wolfie's father, Tiger's mentor, father Earl Woods, loved to teach. He began grooming Tiger for center stage, taking his 2-year-old prodigy on the *Mike Douglas TV Show* to exhibit Tiger's "natural" golf swing in front of the world. It's worth reminding everyone that Tiger's father was a retired United States Army Green Beret, specialized in military training. Like Leopold Mozart, Earl Woods taught intensive work regimens to his son at an extraordinarily early age. Professional golf instruction is said to have begun around four. Future results? Tiger turned pro just before age 21. By 2009 (age 33), he had practiced thirty years and eclipsed nearly every record in golf: 14 Major Championships (2nd best all time), and 71 Professional Golfers' Association Tour wins (3rd best all time). He's racked up $1 billion dollars in tour and endorsement earnings and was the youngest player to win a Grand Slam (*The Masters, U.S. Open, British Open, PGA Championship*).

Does anyone still believe Tiger's accomplishments are the result of good genes alone? Of course not. Tiger routinely credits his father for teaching him to practice with passion and purpose.

Perhaps you've seen Tiger stop a golf swing in full motion if an unexpected roar erupts from the crowd just as he's about to strike the ball. For anyone who's ever golfed, this is no simple task. How does Tiger do that? Earl Woods used to challenge Tiger's mental game by making noises and dropping golf bags during practice swings. How many tour players have prepared since age two, under the eye of a Green Beret? Pressure? Tiger laughs.

The opportunities for little Wolfie and Tiger are well-known. Papa Mozart and Papa Woods dedicated themselves to their child prodigies. The innate skills both kids clearly had were focus, passion, and persistence. These are *Essential*, but not inherently genius or innate. Tiger is clearly kinesthetic which explains precision hand-eye and athletic coordination. He probably could have been world-class at many sports. Wolfie was musical, which explains, well, a lot. He may have been a gifted painter if a brush was put in his hand at age three.

83

So upon close examination of Woods and Mozart, we have to consider that their genius (at least most of it) was disciplined practice for 20 to 30 years.

What do we conclude from all this? In my opinion, no one should feel cheated because they weren't a born genius. Evidence indicates that Mozart and Woods cultivated genius because they had unique opportunities to hyper-focus at the earliest possible age, during formative years, where skill and brain development are at heightened awareness. If anything, what we learn from *geniuses* like Mozart and Woods is that they're flawed human beings like the rest of us. They simply practiced at a single art form longer than most of us ever will.

Note 1: I'm a big fan of Woods and Mozart, so no one should feel this essay takes away from their genius. The primary lesson is that anyone can achieve a degree of genius if they're willing to do the work — to practice with passion and purpose.

Note 2: Psychology experts would likely agree that Woods and Mozart often failed to practice the most basic emotional disciplines, creating an imbalance in their 4 Essentials. Mozart for one struggled socially and financially most of his adult life. Woods struggled with trust and emotions well into his 30s. Values in Woods' arsenal such as integrity, respect, and self-discipline were clearly absent during his fall from grace in late 2009 through 2011. As his golf game and personal life suffered, Tiger stated that "Becoming a better human being would be the key to future success."

Fans and historians can draw their own conclusions.

What About Steve Jobs and Bill Gates?

"I'm convinced that about half of what separates the successful entrepreneurs from the non-successful ones is pure perseverance."
STEVE JOBS (1955 – 2011)
American Entrepreneur, Co-Founder of Apple Computers

Most of us know the stories of Microsoft pioneer, Bill Gates, and Apple visionary, Steve Jobs. They're two of the wealthiest, most recognized figures in history. Volumes have been written about both computer giants so I can offer little more to their biographies. However, there's an interesting lesson I picked up watching one of the 2010 Apple commercials comparing PC to Mac. In a cheeky ad campaign, Apple enjoys poking fun at the many versions of Microsoft's operating systems and history of problems. It's not as if Apple never had to make improvements, but since the PC is known to crash more, the audience gets the joke. The commercial is smart marketing, but I came away with a totally different take than the one Apple intended. The commercial goes something like this:

A young, hip-looking kid in jeans stands next to an older-looking guy wearing a suit and eyeglasses. The hip one is symbolic of Jobs and Mac-lovers, the other of Gates and PC-lovers.

KID MAC: "Hello, I'm a Mac."

PC GATES (SMILING): "And I'm a PC. Hey Mac, did you hear the good news? *Windows 7* is out and it's not gonna have any of the problems that my last operating system had. Trust me."

KID MAC (SUSPICIOUSLY): "I feel like I've heard this before, PC."

For the next 60 seconds, we see PC Gates in progressively outdated leisure suits, insisting each new version of the Microsoft operating software won't have problems of previous versions ...

PC GATES: "*Windows Vista* is here and it won't have any of the problems *Windows XP* had, or any of the problems *Windows '98* had, or any of the problems *Windows '95* had."

By the time the commercial is over, we've flashed back 20 years and PC Gates is now wearing an '80s Miami-Vice-Don-Johnson-wannabe outfit with flip-lens sunglasses. And then comes the final line ...

PC GATES: (winking) "... It's not gonna have any of the problems *Windows 2* had. This time it's gonna be different. Trust me."

What I gleaned from this little history lesson wasn't that Mac was better than PC, or Apple better than Microsoft, or Jobs better than Gates. I've used both PC and Mac. There are pros and cons to both. My epiphany was that Gates and Jobs never stopped innovating. Microsoft was still working out the kinks on *Windows* 7.0 when I wrote this book. The next version won't have any problems of the previous one — trust me.

Gates owned the software industry for decades in spite of glitch after glitch. Why? Passionate innovation. Similarly, Jobs took us through not one, but multiple, technology revolutions. How? He was never satisfied with the first incarnations of his home computer: Apple Lisa, Apple II, or Macintosh. He always wanted his next iteration to be "insanely great." Jobs then rocked our music world by developing i-Tunes. And wasn't that first i-Pod® good enough? Don't be silly. By the time you read this, new versions of iPads® and iPhones® will be in stores. Sadly, Steve Jobs passed away just as I published this book. But his core life lesson lives on. "Think different ... Be persistent."

Both Gates and Jobs are revered as geniuses because they never stopped asking, "What if — how can I make it better?" We classify them as modern-day Mozarts because they innovated with passion and practiced with purpose. For any of us to harness these principles, we can't wonder if our latest effort is good enough. That's easy. It's good enough for today. If the goal is "insanely great," then the genius question is, "What's next ...?"

And the Rest of Us?

Maybe Mozart, Woods, Gates, and Jobs had advantages most of us didn't, like a superior I.Q. or the hyper-focus gene. Perhaps they had the luxury of exceptional mentors, private training, or the best schools. So what? The success formula doesn't end with opportunity — it only starts there. There are plenty of jobless Ph.Ds and gifted artists going nowhere fast. On the flipside, there are challenged people who live extraordinary lives.

Consider Stevie Wonder, Ray Charles, and Andrea Bocelli. Each of these multitalented singers is a blind, Grammy-Award-winning recording artist. In spite of visual impairment, they developed exceptional music and vocal abilities. Did the hindrance of sight hurt their musical genius? I'll leave that one for the reader to ponder.

How about Jay-Z, Lucille Ball, Andre Agassi, Walt Disney, and Abraham Lincoln? What do all these highly successful people have in common? In spite of no college degree, they out-hustled the competition.

What about The Beatles? When John, Paul, George, and Ringo landed on America soil, was it the benefit of a privileged upbringing, or a *"hard days night,"* *"workin' like a dog,"* *"eight days a week?"* Those perfectly choreographed performances were no fluke — The Beatles fine-tuned their act for years in Hamburg, Germany before making a splash in the United States.

As for You and Me, the nurture-versus-nature debate ended a long time ago. Brains, opportunity, and raw talent are never enough. There's a quality of practice and sacrifice that separates world-class musicians, athletes, and entrepreneurs from mere players and pretenders.

If we want something badly enough, practice requires passion and purpose.

Final Thoughts

"Everything is practice."
PELÉ (1940 –)
Brazilian Soccer Legend, 3-Time World Cup Champion, Humanitarian

PERHAPS YOU'RE WRITING A novel, starting a company, or training for the Olympics? If you're serious about being the best, daily improvement is critical. If the great ones teach us nothing else, it's that passion, purpose, *and deliberate practice* are essential for peak performance.

MY 5 PRACTICE RULES

1 Make it fun.
2 Give it 200%.
3 Show up early.
4 Be a passionate student of your game.
5 Assign a focus friend for accountability.
6 Establish written benchmarks and timelines.
7 Build on strengths / neutralize weaknesses.

Connect the Dots

How Practice with Passion and Purpose Connects to The 4 Essentials	
SKILLS	» Passionate practice builds work ethic and self-awareness.
STRATEGIES	» Passionate practice improves focus and goal execution.
VALUES	» Passionate practice requires patience, humility, and discipline.
PURPOSE	» Passionate practice fuels our competitive spirit.

Exercises and Story Contest

1 List your top 3 practice routines for personal and business excellence.
2 Write a story on achievement as a result or practice principles.

RULES AND ENTRY FORM: www.cliffmichaels.com.

Skill 7
Never Quit
Failure is Your Friend

> *"I have not failed.*
> *I've just found 10,000 ways that won't work."*
> THOMAS EDISON (1847 – 1931)
> American Inventor, Scientist, Entrepreneur

Fail Your Way to Success

FROM THE TIME I was 18, I began studying success principles as a means to discover my own career path. I soon realized there were very few people who didn't fail before they achieved success. I was no exception. My failures as a young entrepreneur were extreme. *My Lessons from the Edge* at the front of this book should give you some idea of what I did right and what I learned the hard way.

Bottom line — we all screw up. However, there's a big difference between those who fail, and those who apply lessons from experience. Since our previous chapter covered the importance of passionate practice, this chapter is more about persistence. To inspire your journey, I've selected two men I studied in my late teens. Either could have been Grand Marshall of the Failure Parade.

At the end of this chapter, I've also listed the Adversity Hall of Fame. You'll probably recognize a few names.

The primary lesson is that nothing breeds success like failure.

The Edison Approach

"There's a way to do it better — find it.
Show me a thoroughly satisfied man and I'll show you a failure."
THOMAS EDISON (1847 – 1931)
American Inventor, Scientist, Entrepreneur

M Y FIRST ROLE MODEL on the subject of failure was Thomas Edison. I had just failed a high-school chemistry project when someone called me *Edison* — the master of all failures. I didn't get the joke, so off to the library I went. I soon learned that Edison was the youngest of seven children and didn't learn to speak until he was almost four. When he did, he was a hyper and inquisitive kid (me too). He was so disruptive to an early schoolteacher, that the teacher described Thomas as *too stupid to learn anything*. However, his mother was so sure of young Thomas' abilities, she pulled him from traditional classrooms and opted for home-schooling. Among his early challenges, Edison was not only considered dyslexic, he was technically deaf by his teenage years. His limitations never discouraged him though. To the contrary, he set the bar for generations of innovators.

Fail » Learn » Try again. These were the principles of Thomas Edison, one of the greatest inventors in history. Is it any wonder the first of more than 1000 Edison patents was granted when he was just 22, or that he was the founder of 14 companies, including General Electric? All this, including groundbreaking research in sound recordings, from a child with a learning challenge and hearing impairment. Impossible? Perhaps more insightful than any of his legacies (phonograph, electric automobile, long-lasting light bulbs), Edison left behind a peak-performance playbook.

Like da Vinci, Edison was a fanatic about doodling. From Edison's factory of workers, we discover thousands of papers and notebooks, documenting everything from inventions to business theories. Put it all together and we find a system of intelligent failure. Edison even danced with delight when experiments failed. He worked into the night with teams who shared his passion for trial and error. We see the same willingness to fail in corporate cultures like Google and Starbucks.

Imagine for a moment if each of us adopted Edison's philosophy in all aspects of our lives. Cliché as it may sound, our failures would always be groundbreaking.

Abraham's Arduous Road

*"The path was worn and slippery. My foot slipped from
under me, knocking the other out of the way, but I recovered
and said to myself, 'It's a slip ... and not a fall.'"*
ABRAHAM LINCOLN (1809 – 1865)
American, 16th President of the United States

M Y FIRST YEAR IN college, I read a book titled, *Decision in Philadelphia*. It's an insightful story that captures the triumphs and failures of the Constitutional Convention in 1787. I won't give away too much of the plot you don't already know. The narrative not only depicts the painstaking process of writing the *United States Constitution*, but the many shortcomings of America's Founding Fathers. In the end, some delegates didn't want to sign the *Constitution*. They knew they had failed to abolish slavery or even provide for women's rights. Some considered the *Constitution* a sellout to anyone with black skin. For a country principled in freedom, this disgrace would haunt the Union and lead to civil war three-quarters of a century later.

To remedy one of America's greatest tragedies, it took a man who not only understood failure and adversity, but had an ability to overcome it. This would lead me to study Abraham Lincoln. We know him as the 16th President of the United States, most admirably remembered as a leader who set the instruments in place to abolish slavery and lead his country through civil war. Historians however are far more intrigued by the persistence of a man whose life challenges would have crushed the average soul.

Lincoln was born to humble and tragic beginnings. His parents were uneducated farmers. At age 7, his family was forced from their home. His father was illiterate and his mother died when he was 9. Lincoln's only sister died at child birth a few years later. His grandfather was killed when Lincoln was 23.

At just 24, Lincoln went bankrupt, but good to his word, he spent the next seventeen years paying off debts to friends and colleagues. As a young man, Lincoln failed in business and couldn't get into law school (one of ten U.S. presidents who never graduated from college). Nonetheless, he was self-taught, studied law, and became a lawyer. As an attorney, he had an extraordinary reputation for integrity (Honest Abe). He often encouraged clients not to litigate and accepted less than earned if he believed others would experience financial hardship.

In his mid-20s he was twice defeated in a run for state legislature. At 26, he was engaged to be married, but his first sweetheart died. A broken-hearted Lincoln had a nervous breakdown and battled depression. At 33, he was married to Mary Todd. They had four sons, but three of them died at ages 4, 11, and 18. This was not uncommon in the 19th century, when children died of illnesses we could easily treat today. Imagine being a parent, losing not one, but three children.

Personal tragedy aside, Lincoln's professional career was equally turbulent. At 29, he picked himself up from depression to run for speaker of the state legislature. He was defeated. Although finally elected to the state legislature, Lincoln was defeated several times running for Congress. At 45, he ran for Senate and lost. At 47, he ran for vice president and lost. At 49, he ran for Senate ... and lost *again*.

Historians note that at several stages, Lincoln was likely suicidal (most evident in his late '20s or early '30s). However, his ambition was so honorable, he told friends that life would have no meaning if he hadn't done something worthy of his fellow man.

In spite of all the setbacks, Lincoln pressed on. Then in 1860, age 50, he ran for president, won, and changed the course of history. Today, he is probably the most quoted and revered of U.S. Presidents; remembered as a civil-rights leader, extraordinary statesmen, and mostly, as a man of character. If not for his assassination in 1865, I have no doubt Lincoln had more to teach. But his arduous road to the White House reminds us of his most fundamental lesson:

Never quit. Failure is your friend.

The Adversity Hall of Fame

"Pain is temporary. Quitting lasts forever."
LANCE ARMSTRONG (1971 –)
American Cyclist, Activist, Cancer Survivor

"I have missed more than 9,000 shots in my career. I have lost almost 300 games. On 26 occasions, I have been entrusted to take the game-winning shot ... and I missed. I have failed over and over and over in my life ... and that is why I succeed."
MICHAEL JORDAN (1963 –)
American Basketball Player, 6-Time MVP + NBA Champion

Name & Profession	Failure or Adversity	Ultimate Success
Muhammad Ali Boxer, Humanitarian	Stripped of Championship Title & boxing license in prime of career due to his refusal to fight in the Vietnam War. Ridiculed by government & public.	Recaptured Championship. Became one of the most beloved humanitarians & legendary athletes in the world.
Lance Armstrong Cyclist	Finished last in his first professional race. Diagnosed with cancer in prime of his career.	7-Time Tour de France Cycling Champion. Cancer survivor.
Michael Jordan Basketball Player	Didn't make high-school varsity team as a sophomore – told he was too short.	6-Time NBA Champion. 6-Time League MVP. 2 x Olympic Gold Medalist.
Paul Allen & Bill Gates Co-Founders / Microsoft	Invented Traf-O-Data computer with a tape reader for traffic engineers. Most people never heard of it. It only made a few thousand dollars.	The experience would lead to the creation of Microsoft; the world's leading software company & billionaire status for Allen & Gates.
Albert Einstein Theoretical Physicist	Didn't speak until 4 or read until 7. Described by teachers & parents as slow. Expelled from school.	Discovered Theory of Relativity. Synonymous with genius.
Thomas Edison Inventor	Didn't speak until 4, described by teachers as slow, and had a hearing challenge.	Founder of 14 companies, including GE. Owned over a 1000 patents. Inventor of long-lasting lightbulbs.
Walt Disney Founder, Disney	Fired by news editor for lack of imagination. Went bankrupt. Original theme park was initially rejected by city of Anaheim.	Disney was a pioneer in family entertainment & became one of the most trusted brands in history.

Name & Profession	Failure or Adversity	Ultimate Success
Fred Astaire Actor, Singer, Dancer	First screen test 1933 — Director's memo: "Can't act. Can't sing. Slightly bald. Can dance a little."	76-year career. 31 musical films. Considered one of greatest dancers in history.
Lucille Ball Comedian, Actress	Considered B-List failure in film. Told by drama teachers she had no future in entertainment.	4-time Emmy winner. Pioneering TV executive. Greatest female comedian.
The Beatles Rock 'n' roll Band	Rejected by Decca Records. Told, "We don't like their sound. Groups with guitars are on their way out."	Rock 'n' roll Hall of Fame. Top-selling band of all time.
Charlie Chaplin Director, Actor, Comedian	Rejected by movie studios. Told his pantomime was nonsense.	Pioneered silent film era. Co-Founder of United Artists.
Harland Sanders Founder, KFC	At 65, rejected over 1000 times trying to sell chicken recipe.	KFC became one of most successful food brands and franchises in history.
Winston Churchill British Leader & Orator	Failed 6th grade. Twice failed entrance exam to military academy. Defeated in political races his entire life until age 62.	Prime Minister of England. Nobel Prize in Literature.
Abraham Lincoln Lawyer, Politician	Born into poverty. Haunted by personal tragedies. Defeated for Congress and Vice President.	16th President of United States. Led country through Civil War. Statesmen, civil rights leader.
Charles M. Schulz Cartoonist	His cartoons were rejected by his high school yearbook and he was rejected for a job with Disney.	Creator of *Peanuts* (Charlie Brown), one of the most enduring cartoons of all time.
Jerry Seinfeld Comedian	First time on stage at a comedy club, he froze and was booed off stage.	Returned next night to applause. His show, *Seinfeld*, ran 9 TV seasons, one of the most successful sitcoms in history.
Steven Spielberg Filmmaker	Rejected 3 times by University of Southern California School of Theater, Film and Television.	Oscar-winning director and producer, humanitarian. His films grossed $10 billion worldwide.
Oprah Winfrey Talk Show Host, Producer	Poor and traumatic childhood. Fired from early job as reporter. Told she was "unfit for TV."	Oprah's TV Show ran 25 years. First African-American, female, billionaire & a global brand.

And a Special Tribute to Authors

Name & Profession	Failure or Adversity	Ultimate Success
J.K. Rowling Professional Author	Rowling's *Harry Potter* was rejected by 12 Publishers.	*Harry Potter* became top-selling book and movie franchise.
Stephen King Professional Author	First book, *Carrie*, was rejected by publishers 30 times so he threw the manuscript in the garbage.	King's spouse encouraged him to resubmit and *Carrie* was finally published. King went on to sell millions of novels worldwide with many becoming famous movies.
Richard Bach Professional Author	*Jonathan Livingston Seagull* (JLS) was rejected by publishers 18 times.	*JLS* sold millions of copies since initial publishing in 1972.
Jack Canfield **Mark Victor Hansen** Professional Authors	*Chicken Soup for the Soul* was rejected over 30 times in one month and a reported 140 times before publishing.	*Chicken Soup* book franchise sold over 80 million copies, with over 60 subtitles, in over 30 languages.
Margaret Mitchell Professional Author	*Gone With the Wind* was rejected by publishers 38 times.	Mitchell won a Pulitzer Prize in 1937 and *Gone With the Wind* became a Hollywood treasure.
James Joyce Professional Author	*Dubliners* was rejected 22 times with only 1,250 copies initially printed and only 379 copies sold in 1914. Joyce is said to have purchased 120 of those.	Joyce became one of the most influential writers of the 20th century. *Dubliners* is a classic collection of his best short stories.
Robert Pirsig Professional Author	*Zen and the Art of Motorcycle Maintenance* was rejected by publishers 121 times.	The *Zen* classic sold millions of copies after publishing in 1974.
Richard Hornberger (pseudonym: Richard Hooker) Professional Author	*M*A*S*H* (the novel) was rejected by publishers 21 times.	The book was highly successful and the 1970 Oscar-winning film gave birth to *M*A*S*H*, the longest-running TV series of all time.
Madeleine L'Engle Professional Author	*A Wrinkle in Time* was rejected by publishers 26 times.	Published in 1962, *Wrinkle in Time* became one of the best-selling children's books of all time.
Laurence Peter Professional Author	*The Peter Principle* was rejected by publishers 16 times.	*The Peter Principle* became an iconic business lesson for managers once published in 1969.

Final Thoughts

"It's fine to celebrate success ...
but it's more important to heed the lessons of failure."
BILL GATES (1955 –)
American Philanthropist, Software Pioneer, Co-Founder of Microsoft

Edison, Lincoln, and Disney thrived on failures.
Have you lost enough?

Lance Armstrong saw cancer as yesterday's competitor.
What will you defeat this year?

Stephen King and J.K. Rowling never quit when rejected by publishers.
Did you try again?

Gandhi and Mandela overcame unjust imprisonment.
Are you ready to journey for what you believe in?

Life is sometimes unfair. The world doesn't owe us favors. Intelligence, privilege, and opportunity are not proxies for success. **Persistence rules the day.**

Connect the Dots

How Failure and Adversity Connect to The 4 Essentials	
SKILLS	» Adversity teaches creativity, self-discipline, and crisis management.
STRATEGIES	» Adversity teaches teamwork, leadership, and problem solving.
VALUES	» Adversity teaches humility, patience, and commitment.
PURPOSE	» Adversity teaches us to focus on priorities in life and business.

Exercises and Story Contest

1 List your top 3 failures in life or business and lessons learned.
2 Write an inspirational story on overcoming adversity.

RULES AND ENTRY FORM: www.cliffmichaels.com.

Skill 8
Embrace Challenge and Change

CHALLENGE
"The ultimate measure of a man is not where he stands in moments of comfort, but where he stands at times of challenge."
MARTIN LUTHER KING, JR. (1929 – 1968)
American Civil Rights Leader

CHANGE
"It is not the strongest of the species that survives, nor the most intelligent, but the one most responsive to change."
CHARLES DARWIN (1809 – 1882)
English Naturalist, Theorist

Tackle the Tough Stuff

Any challenges most of us have in life pale in comparison to billions of people suffering worldwide. So here's how I view my good fortune: I had a somewhat dysfunctional childhood (8 schools, 10 homes, divorced parents), but I was lucky compared to most — I didn't starve and had a roof over my head. My hopes of a soccer career were cut short due to injuries — but that led me to entrepreneurial thinking. The real estate market crashed when I left college and I lost everything I worked so hard for — but that inspired me to launch my own company and feed my creative soul. In my late 20s, I ventured into technology. After raising $3 million dollars and working 18-hour days, the dot-com bubble burst and our company failed — we suffered a family tragedy the same year; but I soon discovered greater life purpose.

Through good times and bad, I think most of us learn our greatest lessons through adversity; including the right plans and people to include on our path.

This leads us to 3 immutable laws in life or business:

1 There will be crisis.
2 There will be challenge.
3 There will be change.

From financial setbacks, business hiccups, or family tragedy, adversity will be a test of character and time for courage. It will be a time to build new skills and relationships. It may even be a time to renew purpose. As the cliché goes, "Never miss the opportunity in a crisis."

Analyzing Crisis, Thriving on Chaos

THE OPPORTUNITY IN A crisis begins with awareness of self and surroundings. What are my strengths and weaknesses? What's the mindset of people in my life? What changes are needed? To address these questions, behavioral experts often look at the 5 stages of grief, credited to Swiss-born psychiatrist, Elisabeth Kubler-Ross (1926-2004). The theory was first introduced in her book, *On Death and Dying* (1969).

The Kubler-Ross 5 famous stages of grief are: denial, anger, bargaining, depression, and acceptance. As a method for dealing with trauma or loss, the grief model provides insight to how we deal with crisis or change, each according to personal experience or emotional intelligence.

My own experience with crisis, be it family or business, is that time between stages of grief is not the same for everyone. Some stages are even skipped. Some people jump from denial to depression; suppressing anger. Others regress, going from acceptance back to denial. Nonetheless, understanding these principles is essential, if for no other reason than appreciating what others may be going through and how we might deal with challenges ourselves.

On that note, let's apply the Kubler-Ross model to a global challenge that affected nearly everyone at the same time ...

The Financial Meltdown

In the fall of 2008, a global economic crisis gave birth to shared grief around the world. Not dissimilar to a natural disaster, a financial tsunami left millions in denial, anger, and depression. Fueled by the near collapse of America's banking, auto, and real estate industries, financial ruin rippled across the globe. Before the crisis, many enjoyed prosperity, ignoring pink elephants while economic time-bombs were ready to explode.

When the stock market finally crashed in 2008, the world woke up to tragic flaws in financial systems and government practices. Many had fallen prey to investor schemes, mortgage fraud, and pitfalls of their own greed. Light was soon shed on corrupt practices of major institutions. Unemployment would rise to levels not seen since the Great Depression. Retirement savings were wiped out, illusions of home values stripped away, and years of work destroyed. How would most people deal with the meltdown?

Let's examine the possibilities ...

Stage 1 – Denial

EVERYTHING IS FINE. THIS ISN'T HAPPENING TO ME.

Before the 2008 economic crisis, financial assumptions were often based on a false premise; that parades last forever. These assumptions were rooted in personal greed, non-sustainable debt, and fraudulent accounting practices to name a few — a toxic blend for disaster.

Denial of sound financial principles was the only thing that kept the illusion alive so long. It was months after the crisis hit that Alan Greenspan, former Chairman of the United States Federal Reserve, acknowledged a flaw in his economic theories. He, and most economic experts, foolishly believed business and governments (particularly bankers) would always be honest, regulating themselves in the interest of free and fair markets. World citizens soon joined Wall Street in a state of collective shock.

Denial can't last forever though. If you lose a job or can't pay bills, reality kicks in. Time for Kubler-Ross Stage 2: **Anger**.

Stage 2 – Anger

WHY ME? WHO'S TO BLAME? THIS ISN'T FAIR.

The old expression, "America sneezes and the world catches a cold," was never more apropos than in 2008, only this time, banks and insurance companies had a heart attack. As the world blamed America, angry Americans blamed fat corporations and incompetent government. Truth? Business and political leaders worldwide had turned a blind eye to reckless and corrupt financial behavior for decades. Yet no one was willing to take responsibility for their own irrational exuberance. Nonetheless, serious changes in spending and borrowing would now be imperative. Yikes! Nobody likes change. Time for Kubler-Ross Stage 3: "How can we **Bargain** our way out of this mess?"

Stage 3 – Bargaining

I PROMISE TO BE GOOD. JUST LET ME LIVE TO PLAY ANOTHER DAY.

While no one had perfect solutions to a once-in-a-generation financial storm, the bargaining game of the century began. Everyone looked for handouts, especially banks, insurance companies, and the American auto industry. Individuals and companies alike started **bargaining** for their own survival. Each person was certain their solution was best. At the height of the panic, Lawrence Summers (former Harvard President and Director of National Economic Council for President Barack Obama) said, "There are only two types of economists in today's world; those who don't know, and those who know they don't know." Suddenly, investors realized even the most trusted of financial minds may not know what they're doing. Are we laughing or crying yet? Time for Kubler-Ross Stage 4: **Depression**.

Stage 4 – Depression

I'M BEYOND SAD. I SEE NO SOLUTIONS. NO ONE UNDERSTANDS MY PROBLEM.

For those who lose a job or home, lifestyle interruptions are traumatic. When it occurred on a global scale in 2008, the financial collapse spawned a collective melancholy. The trauma was equivalent to losing a loved one. The manifestations on mind and body were debilitating. For many, **Depression** can paralyze decisions. However, there's always hope. The goal is to move past denial, anger, bargaining, and depression and arrive at Kubler-Ross Stage 5: **Acceptance**.

Stage 5 – Acceptance

I UNDERSTAND. I'M READY TO RECOVER AND TAKE CONSTRUCTIVE ACTION.

The sooner we arrive at **acceptance**, the sooner we can focus on solutions. This is where we've exhausted the previous 4 grief stages and come to a healthy conclusion; that we can gain strength from a negative experience and persevere. This is not only in our self-interest, but for the greater good of those around us.

5 STEPS TO ARRIVE AT ACCEPTANCE

1   Show **humility** and ask for help.
2   Understand the **benefits** of change.
3   Be **optimistic** and trust that there's a way.
4   Be **open-minded** and willing to change habits.
5   Gain **perspective.** Others overcame similar situations.

Handling a crisis requires diligent practice of *The 4 Essentials*, especially humility, teamwork, and self-awareness. We must also empathize and exhibit confidence when others are lost or scared.

As a rule, successful people are a calming force during a crisis. Leadership is their *Essential* asset. They accept challenges as part of life, never allowing chaos to dominate the landscape too long.

So I leave you with this thought on the principle of *acceptance* ...

"Life is about growth and change.
When you are no longer doing that, listen to your whisper."
OPRAH WINFREY (1954-)
. American Talk-Show Host, Entrepreneur, Philanthropist

Final Thoughts

"You must be the change you wish to see in the world."
MOHANDAS GANDHI (1869 – 1948)
Indian Political and Spiritual Leader

WITHOUT THE PERSPECTIVE OF crisis and change, I never could have written this book. For anyone going through a difficult time, the key is getting past denial, anger, bargaining, or depression, and accepting the challenge. Start with questions: Who's been down this road? What strategies will get me forward? What can I learn from the experience?

With a proper mindset, and your 4 Essentials, half the battle is already won.

Connect the Dots

How Challenge and Change Connect to The 4 Essentials	
SKILLS	» Challenges require creativity and self-discipline.
STRATEGIES	» Challenges demand teamwork, leadership, communication, and decision-making ability.
VALUES	» Challenges build courage, character, patience, humility, and gratitude.
PURPOSE	» Challenges create focus on health, family, friends, career, community, and contribution.

Exercises and Story Contest

1 List your top 3 lessons from a crisis, change, or challenge.
2 Write a story on overcoming your toughest challenge in life or business.

RULES AND ENTRY FORM: www.cliffmichaels.com.

Skill 9
Be Ambitious but Recognize Greed

"You can't have everything.
Where would you put it?"
STEVEN WRIGHT (1955 –)
American Comedian

Greed is Good (maybe)

"Greed, for lack of a better word, is good. Greed is right.
Greed works. Greed clarifies, cuts through, and captures the essence of the
evolutionary spirit. Greed, in all of its forms — greed for life, for money,
for love, knowledge ... has marked the upward surge of mankind ..."
MICHAEL DOUGLAS AS GORDON GEKKO
From the movie *Wall Street* (1987) an Oliver Stone Film

The speech was profound. However, there may never have been a more twisted use of the word greed than Gordon Gekko's slick pitch at a shareholder's meeting in Oliver Stone's Oscar-Winning film, *Wall Street*. A stereotype for individual and corporate excess, Gekko is as much the poster child for avarice today as he was in the '80s.

*The following essay is a gentle reminder that healthy ambition is great, but greed, for lack of a better word, is **not** always good.*

Wall Street

IN THE WAKE OF 2008's economic meltdown, Oliver Stone released the sequel to his hit movie, *Wall Street*. My friends and I decided to make a fun night of movie-watching, analyzing both the 1987 original and 2010 sequel. Question of the night: "Were ambition and greed somehow different in the '80s from the 21st century?"

For those who need a refresher on the original *Wall Street*, ambitious but naïve stockbroker, Bud Fox (Charlie Sheen), enters a world of corruption when he pursues a job working for his idol, corporate raider, Gordon Gekko (Michael Douglas). Gekko takes Fox under his wing, but only if Fox will provide illegal, insider information. Enticed by big money, a trophy blonde, and a high-society lifestyle, Fox succumbs to Gekko's spell, the allure of power and profits.

Fox fails to see that Gekko is only using him to destroy Bluestar Airlines, a company where Fox's father works and the source of insider information Fox feeds to Gekko. Once he realizes he's nothing more than a pawn, Fox feels remorse for the damage he's done to those who trusted him, including his father. In a watershed moment about greed, Fox pleads with Gekko not to break up his father's company.

FOX: "When does it all end? How many yachts can you ski behind? How much is enough?"

GEKKO: "It's all about bucks, kid. The rest is conversation ... It's not a question of enough ... It's a zero sum game. Somebody wins. Somebody loses. Money itself isn't lost or made. It's simply transferred ... from one perception to another ... like magic ... the illusion has become real. The more real it becomes, the more desperate they want it ... Capitalism at its finest."

Gekko's calculated response wakes up Fox to the empty life he's chosen. In a last-ditch effort to set things right, Fox double-crosses Gekko but is detected by the Securities and Exchange Commission for insider trading. Jail is the final payoff for Fox and Gekko.

Fast Forward to 2010 >> time to see the sequel, *Wall Street II, Money Never Sleeps*. By the time we left the theater, my friends and I were laughing our heads off at how little things had changed since '87. No need to spoil the flick for those who haven't seen it. Suffice to say, a Gekko doesn't change colors easily.

Our conversation soon turned to schemes of modern day Gekkos, alive and well in the slick suits of crooks like Bernie Madoff. For anyone who missed the broker crime of the century, Bernie Madoff was a modern-day financial advisor who ripped off investors, charities, and the elderly to the tune of billions of dollars. His Ponzi scheme had been going on for decades. Fortunately, Madoff was exposed as a thief in 2009 and jailed for life. *Say hello to Mr. Gekko, Bernie.*

In the end, my friends and I drew a few conclusions about ambition and greed from the *Wall Street* movies:

1 We all have ambition and that's a good thing. The question is whether goals are attached to values. If not, the worst-case scenario may cause an ambitious Fox to sleep with a slimy Gekko. Scary crossbreeding!

2 There will always be Gekkos and Madoffs in the world, screwing innocent victims out of life savings, then feeling no remorse. We can only hope the legal system works when these career criminals are exposed.

So after watching both *Wall Street* films, my friends and I felt we'd reached a few logical conclusions. Primarily, that crooks or sociopaths are sad outliers in society. None of us with ethics and a clear head would allow greed or peer pressure to interfere with honest ambition. I then went home and turned on the television before dozing off to sleep. What game show do you think was on ...?

Deal or No Deal

As if back-to-back *Wall Street* flicks weren't enough, the best lesson in greed came later that night from a comedian, his banker, and their 26 girlfriends.

Hopefully, you've seen the game show *Deal or No Deal*. If not, I'll summarize, then analyze. The show started in the Netherlands in 2002 and was exported to dozens of countries, including the United States. There are slight variations, but I'll stick to the American version. The game is a pop-culture phenomenon where 26 sexy girls in super-tight dresses each hold a sealed, numbered case (1 through 26). Each case has a hidden monetary value inside, between one penny and $1,000,000 dollars.

Follow the player's odds carefully — half the cases (13 of 26) range in value from $.01 cent to $750 dollars. The other 13 cases range from $1,000 to $1,000,000. But 7 of those cases range from $1,000 to $100,000. This means the first 20 of 26 cases have $100,000 or less. Therefore, the odds tilt heavily *against* a contestant trying to win more than $100,000. Only 6 of 26 cases have $200,000 or more. Only 1 case has the $1 million-dollar teaser.

At the beginning of the show, the contestant chooses a sealed case to hold, and then begins opening the remaining 25 cases in rounds of 6, 5, 4, 3, 2, and finally 1 case at a time. With each round, the odds of a contestant's original case having a high-dollar amount increases or decreases, depending on which values have been knocked out. Between rounds, a cash offer is made to the contestant. The game ends when the contestant decides to accept the latest offer. In other words, the show isn't about winning or losing — the contestant is a *guaranteed winner*.

Initial offers tend to be $10,000 to $50,000, but no one ever takes the first or second offer. They don't take the third offer either because it's rarely six figures. This means contestants must risk knocking out 18 of the 26 cases to shoot for bigger offers (the result of a fourth round of case-openings). The longer the game goes on, the higher the risk of knocking out those big dollars.

It's impossible to see what's in the original case selected by the contestant unless *all offers* are rejected, leaving just one other case remaining to compare with the original selection. No one in their right mind does that without a safety net of large numbers remaining, so no one ever has a reasonable shot at winning $1,000,000. It's not complicated. The odds suck against winning more than $100,000. People try and often go home with less than $1,000 after being offered $50,000 to $100,000. Hysterical, right?

Welcome to Psychology 101 — the show is all about risk-assessment under pressure, or more accurately stated, "healthy ambition versus greed." And there's nothing sutble about how the show manipulates the contestant — hot lights, hot girls, and a live, television audience. "Deal or No Deal?" asks host, Howie Mandel, as he takes a call from his imaginary banker, a man sitting in a shadowy cloak of darkness. The banker calculates odds and makes offers to contestants between rounds.

To create a little suspense, the show pauses so Howie and the contestant can chat with friends and family members; asking if they feel the latest offer should be accepted. Meanwhile, the audience screams for greater risk. "No Deal!" As the stakes get higher, Howie even asks contestants if they "have the guts to go all the way?" Hi there — you've just been called out in front of a national, TV audience. The shenanigans are all part of a clever ploy to play on the contestant's ego, greed, and emotions. Common sense is thrown out the window.

So what's the real deal? On January 12, 2006, *The Wall Street Journal* reported several studies about *Deal or No Deal*, conducted by economists who assessed decision-making under risk. The study revealed that contestants take greater risk when they've already seen their highest offer go down, kind of like a poker player who was up $10,000, loses half his money, then believes he can win it back fast. Statistically, we know the longer a player stays in a game of risk, the greater his chances of losing. But game-show contestants get greedy, just like gamblers.

Remember, the contestants on *Deal or No Deal* didn't risk anything, so the idea of winning back lost money is not the same as a gambler who started with his own cash. Contestants are playing with the show's money so their sense of risk is diminished. The study even concluded the biggest losers rejected not only good offers, but would risk everything in an attempt to get closer to what the offer once was. Countless players turn down six-figure fortunes in hopes of something higher, but before the offers get too high, the number of cases remaining are low. This means the odds are greater in final rounds that high numbers *will* get knocked out, causing offers from the banker to plummet.

Should I go for $125,000 while $100,000 is on the table, knowing the next move could cost me $50,000? Smart contestants understand the basic odds and quit before losing a great offer. However, emotional contestants become pure gamblers and lose their minds. It's funny to watch since the show requires zero skill other than common sense. One contestant was offered a choice to go for $1,000,000, having been offered $603,000 with only one other case remaining; the case with $1.00 dollar. Sure enough, he gambled and went home with a buck. It was the biggest bonehead decision in game-show history.

Ironically, my evening dissecting the two *Wall Street* movies ended up with a deeper understanding of ambition and greed after analyzing *Deal or No Deal*. I concluded that greed can affect anyone the same way it does Wall Street tycoons who play with other people's money.

What lesson should we take away? Imagine a stranger comes up to you on the street and offers $100,000 dollars. He then says, "Double or nothing. Deal or no deal? You have 30 seconds to make up your mind." Unless you're independently wealthy and can afford to lose a life-changing offer, don't be a putz ...

Take the deal!

Final Thoughts

"To have little is to possess. To have plenty is to be perplexed."
LAO TSU (6TH CENTURY BC)
Chinese Philosopher

AMBITION IS GOOD. HOWEVER, always pursuing the perfect deal can be a slippery slope. This applies to building a career, negotiating a contract, or launching a business. Greed even applies to our insatiable appetite for knowledge. Case in point — we don't need heavy research statistics for every decision. I'm now whispering to my MBA pals with the lovely spreadsheets and 100-page business plans. In our zeal to know or have it all, the competition may fly right by us. Therefore, greed, for lack of a better word, isn't always good. It may slow us down to the point of utter failure. So remember the entrepreneur's credo:

No matter how ambitious you are, don't let perfect ruin good.

Connect the Dots

How Ambition and Greed Connect to The 4 Essentials	
SKILLS	» Understanding ambition and greed leads to self-awareness, improved decision-making, and superior negotiation skills.
STRATEGIES	» Knowing your limits improves focus, time management, and goal execution.
VALUES	» Mastery of ambition and greed requires patience, humility, and gratitude.
PURPOSE	» A sole focus on money, power, or fame distracts from a balanced life.

Exercises and Story Contest

1 List 3 healthy ambitions you will never compromise.
2 Eliminate at least one element of greed from your life today.
3 Write a story where ambition served you best or greed served you least.

RULES AND ENTRY FORM: www.cliffmichaels.com.

Skill 10
Carpe Diem, Baby!

> *"I went to the woods because I wanted to live deliberately*
> *... to live deep and suck out all the marrow of life."*
> HENRY DAVID THOREAU (1817 – 1862)
> American Poet, Author

Just Do It

You can obtain the finest education and read all the books. You can think positive until you're blue in the face. None of it matters if you don't commit to action. In my favorite film, *Dead Poets Society*, the Latin phrase popularized for that sentiment is **carpe diem!** (seize the day). The modern-day ad campaign for that feeling is **just do it!** (Nike).

Phrase it any way you like — action is the ticket to success.

Lights ... Camera ... Action!

BORN IN CINCINNATI, OHIO, 1946, Steven Spielberg started making 8-millimeter films with friends when he was about 12 years old. However, before he became a motion-picture icon, he was a C-average, high-school student who didn't get accepted to the University of Southern California. Known for its world-class cinema school, USC rejected Spielberg three times and he ended up enrolling at Long Beach State. It would be thirty-five more years before Spielberg received an honorary degree from USC. So what's the true Hollywood story behind the legendary filmmaker's road to success?

As Spielberg recalls in interviews, he was taking the Universal Studios Tour one college summer. He had the nerve to jump off the tour bus, hide behind a sound stage, and stay on the Universal lot all day. He then went to make a phone call and met the head of the Universal film library, Chuck Silvers. Spielberg wasted no time sharing his desire to be a filmmaker. Silvers was so taken with young Steven's passion that he gave the aspiring director a three-day studio pass so he wouldn't have to sneak around.

Spielberg returned the next three days. Each day he would enter through the main gate, showing his pass to the security guard, Scotty. When the pass ran out, Spielberg returned, dressed in a suit and tie, carrying his father's briefcase (filled with nothing but a sandwich). Rather than show the security guard his expired pass, he merely waved to his new friend Scotty, who waved back. Every day, five days per week, for the next three months, Spielberg waved and said, "Hi Scotty," and Scotty let Spielberg through.

For the entire summer, Spielberg hung out on movie sets as an unpaid, intern doing gopher work and honing his craft. Rumors of commandeering his own office are even part of the famous Spielberg tale. As Spielberg proudly shares his early adventures at Universal, he once roamed on to a set where he watched legendary director, Alfred Hitchcock, shoot a film for 45 minutes; that is until young Steven was found out and kicked off the set.

Hollywood fact or fiction? According to insiders, the folklore of Spielberg's Universal backstory began in high school when Spielberg briefly met Silvers through a family connection — Silvers showed the future filmmaker around the studio a bit. Spielberg then reached out to Silvers years later when he jumped off that tour bus. Either way, Spielberg's initiative proved most advantageous; as did the famous 3-day pass. The opportunity that would soon launch his career was just around the corner.

By 21 (1968), Spielberg had written many short scripts, including a 24-minute silent, love story titled *Amblin*. By now, Silvers had introduced Spielberg to a friend who ran a special effects laboratory, Dennis Hoffman. Hoffman saw Spielberg's short films, and agreed to pony up $10,000 to fund *Amblin*. Shortly thereafter, executives at Universal saw Spielberg's work. By 1969, a 22-year-old Spielberg inked a 7-year television deal, making him the youngest director signed by a major studio. Spielberg soon started making TV shows and blockbuster films. The rest is Hollywood history.

Spielberg films have grossed over $10 billion dollars in his 40 years of filmmaking. His Academy-Award winners such as *Schindler's List* (1983) and *Saving Private Ryan* (1998) are only exceeded by his record-breaking box-office adventures such as: *Jaws* (1975) *Raiders of the Lost Ark* (1981), *E.T.* (1982), *Hook* (1991), *Jurassic Park* (1993), *Transformers* (2007). He also co-founded DreamWorks film studio. His philanthropy for art, education, and global causes has been as generous as anyone in Hollywood. *TIME Magazine* also ranked Spielberg as one of the "100 Most Important People of the 21st Century."

An inspiration to entrepreneurs worldwide, Spielberg had no written business plan or college degree when he walked on the Universal Studios lot in the '60s. He was just an average student. What he did have was vision, work ethic, and a healthy dose of chutzpah (that's Yiddish for balls, my non-Jewish amigos). Little Steven was plotting his future since he was twelve, writing stories, making short films, and gaining experience as a novice director. This foundation was many years before Spielberg took the studio tour. When the opportunity struck, the Universal deal wasn't dumb luck. It was the classic Hollywood tale of boy (preparation) meets girl (opportunity).

Warning: *This review has not been rated by the Motion Picture Academy.*

Benefits of Enthusiasm

"Yeah baby, yeah!"
MIKE MYERS (1963 –)
British-Canadian Actor, Comedian, Austin Powers Trilogy (New Line Cinema)

No thanks to reality TV and tabloid journalism, society thrives on drama and negatives. Unfortunately, toxic behavior zaps energy, kills business, and destroys relationships. For that reason, we need balance in the books, shows, and music we feed our souls. The same is true of people we hang out with. For better or worse, it's all contagious. Therefore, if we want to attract like-minded people, it helps to bring some motivational mojo to the scene each day. For the same reason we're attracted to positive people, others will be attracted or turned off by our attitude. It doesn't take more than a smile or kind word to share enthusiasm but the benefits are extraordinary.

So in honor of the guy who put the "yeah" in "yeah, baby, yeah," I suggest sharing the Mike Myers mantra once in a while, famously pitched in *Austin Powers, International Man of Mystery.*

You're switched on! You're smashing! You're shagadelic, baby!

7 Habits of Passionate People

Even if you weren't born with the happy-peppy-super-smiley gene, there are 7 habits of enthusiastic people anyone can adopt. If you can master these tricks of the motivational trade, you'll stay creative and inspire those around you.

HABIT # 1: START AND END THE DAY MOTIVATED
Commit to inspiring routines. Review written goals daily. Read motivational quotes. Hang inspirational art or photos. Listen to your favorite music. Listen to or talk with passionate people.

HABIT # 2: LOVE WHAT YOU DO
You'll be twice as passionate about your day when you genuinely love what you do. If you're not in your ideal job or relationship today, find a way to *add your favorite thing* to each day.

HABIT # 3: SHARE PROGRESS
Keep others motivated by sharing progress. If it's hard see the finish line, people tend to quit. Give credit where due and inspire next steps.

HABIT # 4: MAINTAIN A HEALTHY MIND, BODY, AND SOUL
Unhealthy routines lead to stress, low energy, and poor health. Enthusiasm is driven by the positive fuel we feed our mind, body, and soul. Exercise. Eat well. Find balance.

HABIT # 5: SURROUND YOURSELF WITH ENTHUSIASTIC PEOPLE
Our energy will rise to the level of our peers. If your motivational meter is low, develop a routine that includes friends who share your passions.

HABIT # 6: ASSIGN YOURSELF A MOTIVATIONAL SERGEANT
The best athletes have trainers. The best teams have inspirational coaches. Successful companies have motivational leaders. Make a pact with a focus friend or co-worker to inspire and hold each other accountable every day.

HABIT # 7: MAKE IT FUN
Smiles + Laughter = Success (bonus points for goofy).
Math skills not required.

P.S. Small is the New Big

There are many books and motivational gurus pitching "Think BIG." Generally, it's good advice and inspirational. However, if we only think BIG, we can easily sabotage little missions. In fact, the mantra *Go BIG or go home* may be the worst advice you ever get. For example, people fail more often than they succeed biting off more than they can chew. A BIG focus often requires small details. If it's true that less is truly more, then BIG purchases tend to waste money and clutter space. Do you really need to leave that HUGE carbon footprint?

In the business world, many entrepreneurs never get off the ground because the BIG idea requires BIG money or the BIG partner. Sometimes it's better to start with baby steps. First prove the idea, build relationships, make a few sales; then attract bigger clients and investors.

Also think about your personal banwidth or ability to handle chaos. Are you sure you want BIG budgets, BIG payrolls, and the bureaucratic committees that go with them? Many of us prefer less waste, bigger profits, and small teams that make fast decisions.

Some of the most successful lifestyles and profitable business models are virtual, streamlined, and outsourced. So if intimate is more your style, don't feel pressured to go BIG. The headaches of BIG companies may drive you nuts. Ask yourself, "What do I really need for health, wealth, and happiness?" If smaller makes you happy, go for it! Less chaos and less stress can be just as rewarding.

Yes, think big and carpe diem, baby!
But consider staying lean ... small really is the new big.

Final Thoughts

"Entrepreneurs don't always ask permission.
Sometimes they ask forgiveness."
ANONYMOUS

- Talk is cheap. **Just do it!**
- Stop blaming others. **Just do it!**
- The world doesn't owe you a favor. **Just do it!**
- You don't need to check with 20 friends. **Just do it!**
- It's the pursuit of excellence, not perfection. **Just do it!**
- Star athletes don't think when they're in the zone. **Just do it!**
- Life is what you make it. Want yours to be extraordinary? **Just do it!**

Connect the Dots

How Enthusiasm Connects to The 4 Essentials	
SKILLS	» Enthusiasm enhances performance.
STRATEGIES	» Enthusiasm is critical to teamwork, relationships, communication, and leadership.
VALUES	» Enthusiasm builds courage and commitment.
PURPOSE	» Enthusiasm attracts like-minded friends, peers, and mentors.

Exercises and Story Contest

1. List 3 ways that you bring daily mojo to life and the workplace.
2. Take 3 **new** action steps to **seize the day** on **today's mission**.
3. Write an inspirational story on the spirit of carpe diem.

RULES AND ENTRY FORM: www.cliffmichaels.com.

Congratulations!

You've just concluded a first step toward a **Master's** in **Basic Abilities.**

Recap: The 10 Basic Life Skills

1 **Define success** by your standards, not the measure of others.

2 Unleash your **entrepreneurial soul.**

3 Build a passion for **learning.**

4 Master the art of **leverage** through **tools** and **mentors.**

5 **Cultivate** curiosity and creativity.

6 **Practice** with passion and purpose.

7 Never quit. **Failure is your friend.**

8 Embrace **challenge** and **change.**

9 **Ambition** is good. **Greed** has pitfalls. Know the difference.

10 Enthusiasm is contagious. **Carpe diem, baby!**

Essential 1 — Freshman Degree

This diploma certifies that the reader of this book
has attained an honorary degree in Basic Life Skills.

Continue through *The 4 Essentials*
to graduate with a **Master's** in **Basic Abilities**

Essential # 2: **Action Strategies**

*"All the passion in the world won't matter
if you're running east looking for a sunset."*
ANTHONY "TONY" ROBBINS (1960 -)
Speaker, Entrepreneur, Performance Strategist

Connecting Skills with Action

ACTION STRATEGIES ARE GUARANTEED to accelerate personal growth and career development. Once you've connected these *Essentials*, your life, team, or business mission will be supercharged.

After all, what good are skills, values, or purpose without strategies?

THE 7 ACTION STRATEGIES

1   Self-Discovery and Team Mission

2   Emotional, Social, and Communication Intelligence

3   Relationships and Networking

4   Decision Making and Problem Solving

5   Teams · Leaders · Advisors

6   Focus and Time Management

7   Hardcore Goal Execution

Strategy 1
Self-Discovery
and Team Mission

"To be yourself in a world that is constantly trying to make you something else is the greatest accomplishment."
RALPH WALDO EMERSON (1803 – 1882)
American Poet, Philosopher

Youthful Optimism

A S KIDS, WE HAD a special gift — no fear. We jumped on that bike and started pedaling. If we were lucky, we not only discovered what we could do, but what we were good at. For me, it was soccer. I started as a goalkeeper but shots would fly right over my head. Fortunately, I discovered speed as my unique ability and a great asset for driving past defenders. As a result, I scored my share of goals and played for championship clubs through childhood.

I had a similar awakening as a young entrepreneur. I learned early on that anything was possible if I matched the right ambition and abilities. So when I embarked on a business career with no formal training or college degree, I tried different things. In the end, networking and negotiating deals exercised my verbal skills. Remodeling homes fueled my creative side. Launching companies unleashed my adventurous soul.

When I look back at the first 20 years of my adult life (18-38), the thing that served me best was self-discovery. If I strayed too far from my passion or strengths, success was harder to come by. Today, all my research draws the same conclusion — a little introspection and a whole lot of youthful optimism have common threads with successful people.

I can further illustrate these principles with my favorite baseball story ...

Are You a Pitcher or Slugger?

A young boy from an orphanage once approached home plate at an empty baseball field. Alone, carrying his bat and a ball, the boy looked to center field and shouted, "I'm the world's greatest home-run hitter!" He then tossed the ball in the air, swung his bat, and missed. "Strike one," he announced to his imaginary fans. He then picked up the ball and shouted even louder, "I'm the world's greatest home-run hitter!" He tossed the ball in the air, then swung, and missed again. "Strike two," he calmly said. Finally, the boy pointed his bat to center field, and with the fierce look of a big-league slugger, shouted at the top of his lungs, "I'm the world's greatest home-run hitter!!!" He tossed the ball in the air, swung with all his might, and missed again. "Strike three." Finally, the boy reflected, smiled wide, and whispered ...

"What do you know ... I'm the world's greatest pitcher."

MORAL OF THE STORY: We may strike out a few times discovering our unique ability, but with optimism, we'll always see the positive side of failure.

Now for the million-dollar question:
Which famous ballplayer do you think that kid grew up to be?

Hardcore fans know that baseball's home-run king, Babe Ruth, may have been one of the greatest pitchers of all time if not for the fact *he was the greatest home-run hitter in the world.* Initially scouted from St. Mary's Industrial School for Boys in Baltimore, Maryland, Ruth started his career as a pitcher with the Boston Red Sox, posting prolific records for years. He had 18 wins in 1915, 23 wins in 1916 (with 9 shutouts), and 24 wins in 1917. As a pitcher, Ruth even won 3 World Series games without a loss. He also had a 29-1/2 scoreless-inning streak in Series appearances. At one time, Ruth really was *the greatest pitcher in the world!*

But in 1919, Ruth also set a major league record with 29 home runs. His unique skill as the greatest home-run hitter made it impossible for him to remain the greatest pitcher. Why? Pitchers need to rest their arms and can't play every day. So, with his personal stock rising as a slugger, Ruth was traded to the New York Yankees where his unique home-run ability could be put to better use. Then in 1920, Ruth became a full-time Yankee outfielder, hit 54 home runs, and batted .376 (extraordinary, even by modern standards). In 1923, Ruth even hit .393 a Yankee record that may never be broken. The rest is history. Ruth rewrote baseball's record books, setting the all-time home-run mark (714), a record that lasted nearly half a century. On the road to 714 homers, Ruth also struck out 1,330 times, proving again that success often requires failure.

P.S. Don't Peter-Principle Yourself

Once you've discovered your unique ability, it's a good idea to delegate, collaborate, or eliminate stuff you don't know, don't do well, don't like, or don't have time for. I repeat this mantra often — and for good reason.

In 1968, a theory was developed by Dr. Laurence Peter called *The Peter Principle*. The theory explains the fatal flaw of promoting someone based solely on job competence or seniority. In his study, Peter discovered that skills demanded for a new job position are often different from skills required in a previous position. In other words, people may rise to the level of their incompetence. They might even create a lifestyle counterproductive to goals, passion, or ability.

To illustrate the *Peter Principle*, let's spotlight Jim, a passionate car salesman. For his 10 years as top sales guy, Jim's firm promotes him to manager. He'll now get a hefty raise and bonus override on 10 other salespeople. His income could jump from $100,000 to $120,000 per year. Jim will be responsible for managing meetings and the sales team. This all sounds good but after six months, Jim realizes he hates managing people (especially salespeople). Within a year, Jim's personal clients have been neglected and company sales have plummeted. He also misses the fun factor in his life. His golf game is in the toilet and he has no time for friends, family, or fitness. His world is now one bundle of managing headaches. Worse, Jim's stress level is up and quality of life is down. Was the promotion worth it? Not for Jim. Some folks are salespeople, others are managers, and the two don't always match. After a year of frustration, Jim returned to sales where he and his company were infinitely happier; and making more money.

THE LESSONS ARE OBVIOUS:

1 If you're thinking of change, don't Peter-Principle yourself.
2 Careers must be aligned with passion, purpose, and abilities.
3 Never promote someone to the level of their incompetence.

In most cases, by sticking to what we know best, and allowing others do the same, we'll accomplish more, with less grief, in half the time, and at lower costs.

Ready ... Fire ... Aim!

Now that self-discovery is on our radar, imagine a scenario where a coach calls one set of plays, but players execute from a different playbook. Imagine further that the coach and players don't know each other's strengths or weaknesses because they never practice on the same field or even at the same time. In this Bizarro world I've just described, players and coaches don't even know each other's names. Sound far fetched? Don't laugh. It happens every day in companies where colleagues and collaborators work on different floors, different cities, even competing countries. There's often a huge disconnect from person to person and office to office. Clock in, off we go, why we do it, nobody knows. This is a shame since individual and team goals must be in harmony for peak performance. If just a few alignments are out of whack, even talented people with great skills and strategies can sabotage one another.

As a corollary to the above, I developed a 12-point system for self-discovery and team analysis. The system can drill down on anything from strengths and career goals to business vision and corporate culture. The approach is simple and works equally well for individuals, teams, and leaders. It also puts the best people in the right positions to save time, money, and effort. In chapters to follow, we'll discuss complimentary strategies like communication, teamwork, and hardcore goal execution.

The 12–Step Discovery System

Review these questions with your inner circle.
For teams, replace "I or me" with "we or our."

An E-course and Tools to help with this system are at: www.cliffmichaels.com

Discovery Steps	Starter Questions
1 Define Success	» What makes me happy and why?
2 Discover Your Passion	» What do I love to do?
3 Discover Personality Type	» Am I verbal, visual, logical, athletic, musical, creative, self-aware, socially savvy?
4 Discover Strengths	» What assets do I have? (skills, teams, resources, experience)
5 Discover Weaknesses	» What liabilities do I have? (gaps or inexperience)
6 Discover Opportunities	» Could opportunities be risks?
7 Discover Threats	» Could threats be opportunities?
8 Discover Unique Ability	» Where should my focus be?
9 Discover and Prioritize Goals	» What matters most and when do I want it?
10 Define Your Mission	» What do I do, who do I do it for, and why?
11 Define Your Vision	» What is the future aspiration of my mission?
12 Discover Core Values	» What values support my mission and vision?

Focus on # 9

Once you've discover your goals, categorize and prioritize them.

Fun · Health · Finance · Business · Projects · Relationships · Learning

---

We'll expand on hardcore goal execution in chapters to follow.

Final Thoughts

"The highest form of human excellence is to question oneself and others."
SOCRATES (469 BC – 399 BC)
Greek Philosopher

I'M A BIT CLAUSTROPHOBIC. As a result, I nearly missed one of the most thrilling experiences of my life. In 2003, I was on a trip to the Great Barrier Reef in Australia. Scheduled for a 4-day dive with friends, the notion of confined breathing under ocean water had me spooked. I had scuba trained in a swimming pool months earlier but even that was scary. By the time I arrived in Australia, I was ready to snorkel, giving up the fantasy of scuba diving.

My friends however knew I was on this trip as part of a self-discovery mission. So they had the dive master set aside time for private lessons along the shore. Later that day we took to sea. My pals literally formed a circle around me in the water, held my hand, and took me underwater a few feet at a time. Before I knew it, I was on the ocean floor (80 feet deep). I saw colors and creatures I never imagined. I was feeding giant cod fish by hand. I was eye-to-eye with sharks, rays, and sea turtles. It was a great lesson in humility.

From that day on, I've always believed that self-discovery is analogous to snorkeling versus scuba diving. We can peek a few feet below the surface or explore a much deeper world filled with insight and adventure.

For those looking to shake things up, I propose the scuba diver's mindset. The more ambitious the mission, the more essential it will be to rope in friends and advisors, maybe someone to hold your hand. For teams, group exercises will drive smarter leadership, insightful marketing, and better growth strategies.

As the next six chapters illustrate, a variety of action strategies are highly connected to the self-discovery process.

Connect the Dots

How Self-Discovery Connects to The 4 Essentials	
SKILLS	» Self-discovery builds focus and shores up weaknesses.
STRATEGIES	» Self-discovery improves decisions, communication, teamwork, leadership, and relationships.
VALUES	» Self-discovery requires patience, humility, and, integrity.
PURPOSE	» Self-discovery defines who we are, what we want, and why we want it.

Exercises and Story Contest

1 Answer the 12 self-discovery questions. Go scuba diving, not snorkeling.
2 Brainstorm your mission, vision, and values with closest peers.
3 Create a personal *and* business mission statement.

CLIFF'S PERSONAL MISSION
"Love, learn, live, and give with passion, humility, and gratitude."

CLIFFMICHAELS.COM BUSINESS MISSION
"Inspire, give back, and raise the bar for education and entrepreneurship."

RULES AND ENTRY FORM: www.cliffmichaels.com.

Strategy 2
Emotional, Social, and Communication Intelligence

> *"The emotional mind is far quicker than the rational mind, springing into action without pausing even for a moment to consider what it's doing."*
> DANIEL GOLEMAN (1946 –)
> American Psychologist, Author, Journalist

What Drives Us

SOCRATES SAID, "KNOW THYSELF." From Greek philosophers to modern-day psychologists, we've been examining human behavior for thousands of years. Why? The ability to know ourselves and read others is critical to success. This is as true for relationships and conflict resolution as it is for negotiations, leadership, and team building. To that end, let's recap two life skills we touched on back in *Essential 1, Skill 3: Build a Passion for Learning.*

1 **Emotional Intelligence:** Our self-awareness, self-discipline, and ability to manage emotions. This is a basic understanding of *what drives me.*

2 **Social Intelligence:** Our ability to empathize, get along, and read situations. This is a basic understanding of *what drives other people.*

Considering the importance of these skills, have you ever wondered why people often miss subtle clues that would tell them we're happy or frustrated? Perhaps it's the cold-hearted doctor with poor bedside manners? Maybe it's the dictatorial CEO with a Napoleon complex who thrives on big words and silent stares? Sometimes we forget that a simple smile (or lack of one) sends a powerful signal.

But even if we make our best effort, we can't possibly know what someone is feeling all the time or the depth of their life experience — we're not in their head or shoes. At the very least, there's a lot we don't know and that's step one of being socially intelligent. A person may have a physical or emotional challenge we need to appreciate. Their home or workplace could be dysfunctional. So if we're interested in genuine relationships (personal and professional), we have to be willing to learn a little about what motivates someone; not only based on their past experience, but what might drive them tomorrow.

From Psychology 101, we know that motivational drivers are common for all of us, starting with basic instincts (sex, food, health, safety, security). For others, nothing is more important than family, friends, love, or a sense of belonging. How about career, money, or personal passions? Many are also guided by altruistic values, hoping to make a difference in the world.

The challenge: Few of us have the same motives, at the same time, or with the same priority. This puts a lot of people in potential conflict every day.

The solution: Sorry, no shortcut here. Building emotional (self) and social (people) intelligence is a daily process; but rewards are immeasurable.

So how did most of us develop our people skills? For some, social abilities are innate. We say, "that guy is a born salesman" or "that girl is a people pleaser." But even if som one is highly social or verbal, they may not *connect* well with others. Many extroverts talk too much. The result? They fail to listen, misread situations, or turn people off. On the flipside, seemingly shy people often rank very high on the emotional *and* social intelligence scale. The "shy ones" often make the best listeners, giving them a potential leg up on extroverted peers. In the end, listening, learning, and sharing experiences are critical to success.

Biologically and neurologically, what we eat and drink is equally important to our thinking skills. The same is true of sleep and exercise – the books we read – the games we play – the shows we watch – the friends we keep – or the stress we create. It all affects brain function, body chemistry, mood swings, and energy levels. Consequently, our ability to self-reflect or relate to others is highly connected to what we feed our mind, body, and soul.

Having said all that, there are simple strategies anyone can employ to improve both self-awareness and people skills. If we take just a little time to understand what drives people (including ourselves), it's easier to build trusted relationships, productive teams, and satisfied customers.

136

We all get busy so it's very easy to miss signals or send the wrong ones. For example, did you ever roll your eyes at the lovely barista who got your coffee order wrong; making someone the victim of your dysfunctional moment? Yes, I'm talking to you, Mr. Grande-Double-Mocha-Cappuccino-Soy-Latte with an extra shot of crazy! We don't realize the effect our words and actions have sometimes (even the simple roll of our eyes). That's precisely why we need to be more self-aware and socially conscious. So as we move to our next action strategy (communication), let's bring emotional and social intelligence along for the ride. These are *Essential* skills none of us can do without — especially when we're caffeinated.

He Said, She Said

*"The most important thing in communication
is to hear what isn't being said."*
PETER DRUCKER (1909 – 2005)
Austrian Professor, Author of 39 books including *Innovation & Entrepreneurship*

It's one thing to be intelligent or have an ability to read people. It's a whole other ball game to communicate well. In fact, communication skills are so inherently linked to success strategies, it's a bit mind-boggling that career-training programs don't give this discipline greater attention. In my experience, this is where a paradigm shift in real-world education could easily begin.

Consider carefully that every e-mail, conversation, or visual image, has the awesome power to change lives — for better and worse we can:

- Inspire or discourage others
- Negotiate or lose a deal
- Build or destroy relationships
- Mitigate or escalate conflicts
- Read people or miss the signs

With technology, cell phones, and social media at the core, it's easier than ever to communicate well or screw things up really fast. We asked for speed but sure enough, digital mania has been a blessing and a course. The question is, have you mastered these new tools for better or worse?

Say What?

> Tweet-Tweet **Twitter** bird. Can you **Digg** it? **Facebook** me, but whatever
> you do, don't take up all **MySpace**. Are you **Linked-In**? Check my **blog**,
> go **YouTube** yourself, and let's **Skype** after you **ping** me, baby!

If any of the above jargon sounds foreign to you, welcome to 21st century cyberspeak. Consider today's communication tools (phone, e-mail, text, online networks). We don't always get to read body language, hear voice inflection, or see facial expressions. As a result, some of our key life skills don't get the practice they deserve. However, when anyone discusses success principles, the conversation invariably turns to communication and people skills — an ability to resolve conflicts, play nicely, and convey clear messages is critical, whether we're courting love, selling widgets, or collaborating ideas. Unfortunately, something funky happened with the birth of cell phones and Internet nirvana.

With keyboards racing at light speed, **what** we say is just as relevant as **how, where, when, why**, and to **whom** we say it. These days, we're on record with every text, post, or photo, but are messages clear, consistent, and constructive? Do we give thought to words or unleash a verbal arsenal every chance we get? Have we factored in the Facebook and Twitter Effect?

Obviously, you can't walk around paranoid. If your life is an open book, then post away — be wild, sexy, funny, or provocative. However, don't be disappointed if the world doesn't get your brand of humor or politics. Peers may not appreciate everything we slap online. We may think an innocent comment or photo won't be taken out of context, but in cyberspace, all bets are off. We can easily damage reputations in seconds, including our own. I'm not saying we have to filter everything, but as Abraham Lincoln said, "It's better to remain silent and be thought a fool than to open one's mouth and remove all doubt."

Sometimes Silence "is not" Golden

On the other hand, you may be familiar with a classic line from the movie, *Cool Hand Luke* (1967)? "What we have here is a failure to communicate." For many people, a psychological defense mechanism for dealing with uncomfortable situations is to simply go silent. Here's the problem — there's no faster way to alienate someone than a failure to communicate. This includes using text or email to avoid a phone call or face-to-face conversation. Many people are completely aware when they're doing this. Others do it subconsciously. Either way, the elephant in the room won't go away. Letting someone know we heard their concern and will do our best to address things is far better than no response, or worse, a misleading one.

Conclusion: *Communication skills matter more than ever, especially in a digital world. If we agree on these principles, let's now connect our emotional and social intelligence with communication intelligence.*

The 12 Communication Commandments

COMMANDMENT # 1: MASTER THE ART OF LISTENING
We were probably given two ears and one mouth for a reason. We learn far more from what we hear than what we say. Only through listening can we communicate well.

COMMANDMENT # 2: COMMUNICATE WITH INTEGRITY
In his classic book, *The 4 Agreements*, Don Miguel Ruiz suggests that we are best served if we are "impeccable with our word." Since I can't improve on the wisdom of Ruiz, I echo his famous sentiment: "Speak with integrity, say what you mean (do what you say), avoid speaking against yourself or others, and use the power of your word for truth."

COMMANDMENT # 3: CONSIDER THE FACEBOOK AND TWITTER EFFECT
We have to know our audience, especially if we're building a personal or company brand. There's an enormous difference between whispering a dirty joke to an old friend versus posting a memo for the world to see.

COMMANDMENT # 4: FOCUS ON FIRST IMPRESSIONS
It was Dale Carnegie who said, "A person's name is to that person the sweetest and most important sound in any language." So smile, find common ground, and use someone's name often. We get one shot at first impressions.

COMMANDMENT # 5: SHOW RESPECT AND MASTER CIVIL DISCOURSE
Speak softly, admit when you're wrong, and try to take the higher ground. It's to your advantage to let the other person go first. Gathering information before speaking is a standard for comminication excellence.

Commandment # 6: Never Assume

The old joke about the word "assume" is that we never want to make an "Ass" out of "U" and "Me." So don't assume gender, race, or social status tell us anything about someone's experience or intelligence. Don't assume people get you. Communication requires listening, learning, and sharing.

Commandment # 7: Don't Fail to Communicate

Silence can be tragic. Countless relationships and projects fail because no one shared knowledge or an opinion. Speak up or suffer the consequences.

Commandment # 8: Be Specific

The popular acronym for sales, goal-setting, and communication excellence is to be **S.M.A.R.T.**

Specific • **M**easurable • **A**ttainable • **R**elevant • **T**ime-oriented

If you want specific results, you need specific communication.

Commandment # 9: Manage Expectations

There's an old Gaelic proverb that says, "He who promises most will perform least." The modern catch-phrase for that sentiment is, "Under promise and over deliver."

Commandment # 10: Consider Your Delivery Options

Private or public? Online or offline? Formal or informal? Will your words be recorded (text, audio, video)? Choose the medium wisely.

Commandment # 11: Practice Humility and Gratitude

Three simple words will make you the world's most gracious communicator. **Please** and **Thank you.**

Commandment # 12: Grade Yourself Now and Then

What exactly did you communicate in all those posts, e-mails, and conversations? Check the content for word choice, brand awareness, and social intelligence.

Final Test > Was your communication clear, consistent, and constructive?

Can Anyone Be a Great Communicator?

I'm often asked if some people are born with communication intelligence such as great speakers, charismatic leaders, or passionate entrepreneurs. The answer is "Yes." However, while the gift of gab is a wonderful pet, people with less than perfect verbal skills can be equally great communicators. As mentioned earlier, great listeners are often better received than their loquacious peers. This means successful communication is as much art as science.

Speaking of science, read the next essay and you should be convinced that "anyone" can be a great communicator.

Find Your Voice

> *"Intelligence is the ability to adapt to change."*
> STEPHEN HAWKING (1942 –)
> British Theoretical Physicist

When we consider the world's great communicators, it's easy to point to inspirational CEOs or heads of state. However, I'm especially grateful to one man for giving the world his unique gift of speech.

Born in 1942, British theoretical physicist, Stephen Hawking, is best known for his breakthroughs in cosmology and quantum physics. Not since Einstein has someone captured our imagination over little things — like black holes or the history of the universe.

Hawking is a rock star in the world of science. Over thirty years, he was the Lucasian Professor of Mathematics at the University of Cambridge. His book, *A Brief History of Time: From the Big Bang to Black Holes,* sold more than 9 million copies and was on the *British Times* bestseller list over four years.

Beyond the cosmos, Hawking is an inspiration to millions for his courage and unique communication style. In 1962, shortly after he earned his B.A. at Oxford, Hawking developed symptoms of amyotrophic lateral sclerosis (aka: *Lou Gehrig's disease*), named after New York Yankees' Hall-of-Fame first baseman. The disease left Hawking almost completely paralyzed, but that's just half the story. In 1985, Hawking had a bout with pneumonia that threatened his life and limited breathing capacity. An emergency tracheotomy was performed and Hawking lost the ability to speak. He has since used a voice synthesizer to communicate.

In spite of paralysis and voice loss, Hawking continued to communicate revelations of the universe with his stellar wit and galactic wisdom for half a century. The upshot is that the British Hawking uses a voice synthesizer that has an American accent. When asked why he never considered a different voice, Hawking said he had never heard one better. It just goes to show, we can each find our unique voice.

What if Someone Can't See, Hear, or Speak?

Let's not forget Helen Keller (1880 – 1968). She was the first deaf-blind student to earn a Bachelor of Arts at 24 from Radcliffe College. She went on to inspire millions as a prolific writer, social activist, and symbol of courage. Never able to master speech due to inadequate teaching methods in her time, Keller still exceeded a range of communication ever imagined for someone so seemingly challenged. In her lifetime, she published books, toured the world, and became a teacher herself. She met every President of the United States from Coolidge to Kennedy, and, like Hawking, won the Presidential Medal of Freedom for her social and humanitarian efforts.

Final Thoughts

*"It's more fun to talk with someone who doesn't use long,
difficult words but rather short, easy words like, 'What about lunch?'"*
WINNIE THE POOH (1926 –)
Fictional Bear, Created by A.A. Milne, Adapted by Disney

CONSIDERING ANY SUCCESS I'VE had in life or that of peers I admire, the most common thread has often been tied to communication and people skills. When we're able to get along, make friends, bridge gaps, and resolve conflicts, life is simpler. In fact, there may be nothing more crucial to improving global education than connecting programs for social, emotional, and communication intelligence.

Connect the Dots

How Emotional, Social, and Communication Intelligence Connect to The 4 Essentials	
SKILLS	» Emotional, social, and communication intelligence accelerate learning and trust-building ability.
STRATEGIES	» Emotional, social, and communication intelligence are critical to relationships, teamwork, leadership, and conflict resolution.
VALUES	» Emotional, social, and communication intelligence require patience, humility, integrity, respect, and tolerance.
PURPOSE	» Emotional, social, and communication intelligence provide keys to live, work, and play with anyone, anytime, anywhere.

Exercises and Story Contest

1 List your top 3 strategies for communication excellence.
2 Write a story about communication or social media and lessons learned.

RULES AND ENTRY FORM: www.cliffmichaels.com.

Strategy 3
Relationships and Networking

> *"You can make more friends in two months by becoming really interested in other people than you can in two years by trying to get other people interested in you. Which is just another way of saying that the way to make a friend is to be one."*
> DALE CARNEGIE (1888 – 1955)
> American Writer, Lecturer, Success Trainer

Build a Solid Foundation

Each of us was taught something about relationships by the people in our lives. Be it a friend, lover, co-worker, or customer, the key has always been that quality relationships take time and effort. We can't fake it or expect more than we give. Successful people in particular work very hard at developing long-term relationships on solid foundations.

5 PILLARS OF HIGHLY SUCCESSFUL RELATIONSHIPS

1 Mutual respect
2 Trust and loyalty
3 Honest communication
4 Passion, fun, and humor
5 Commitment and consistency

If your personal or professional relationship needs a booster shot, be sure to double-check the 5-point rubric above. It's guaranteed therapy!

145

Defining Quality Relationships

I ONCE SPOKE TO a group of 200 college students and asked their definition of "a relationship." Rapid-fire responses bounced off the walls from friend, family, lover, to client, colleague, and mentor. Responses included positive elements like trusted, romantic, or profitable. Others were negative, such as destructive, codependent, or counterproductive. Equally insightful were questions like: "Which relationships are most important and why? Should focus be on family, coworkers, or social networks? How about the 20% of clients who make up 80% of our business?"

Conclusion
*"The importance of each relationship
depends on your focus in life and business."*

When many of us look back at our happiest or most successful moments, more often than not we're talking about *quality* relationships. Not including our loyal Facebook friends, how many people can we rely on at 3:00 a.m.? No less important, can they rely on us?

Quality relationships begin with people we call family, friends, partners, and clients — the folks who enrich our lives, keep things fun, and drive our competitive spirit. So it's not about whether the goal is to meet new people, make a million dollars, or save the planet. It's about starting with one *quality* relationship; then developing a small group who trust one another. From there, if we do it right, there's no limit to the *quality or quantity* of relationships we can build.

Network with a Purpose

Friends know me as a networker. I enjoy connecting with people. When I'm at my best, I'm introducing peers and listening to stories. That curiosity and willingness to help others comes back in many ways. The fact that I'm verbal doesn't hurt. As discussed however, talking too much can interfere with anyone's ability to hear. Having attended countless social and business events worldwide, I've therefore drawn this conclusion:

*The best networkers are not big talkers.
They are, more often than not, the very best listeners.*

If networking is your goal, consider this exercise at your next social or business gathering — *simply observe people carefully*. Watch folks stick to their clique as if their identity depends on it. Others schmooze, collect cards, but never really connect; this is often true of salespeople who focus only on themselves or their product. Then there's the problem child; enamored with their cell phone more than the person they're talking to; there's nothing more irritating than a conversation with someone looking down (texting or e-mailing) rather than looking you in the eye. For anyone who missed the memo, a cell phone during a serious face-to-face conversation is a major faux pas.

The behavior patterns above are common, even fun to watch, especially if we just came to see the people show or hang out with friends. However, if meaningful relationships are the goal (social or business), there's a much smarter and profitable approach.

In every crowd there are highly successful networkers and you know them the second you meet them. They smile and listen well. They make people feel welcome. They introduce strangers to one another. They treat everyone with respect. When you see these people, don't be intimidated. They want you to say, "Hello." They live for "Hello."

At their core, strong networkers view everyone as an equal peer, valued client, and potential friend. They're always curious, caring, and connecting — these are the principles I've learned from social entrepreneurs, famous political leaders; even strangers at funky Halloween parties. So if you care to be a card-carrying member of this VIP club, the rules of engagement are on the next page.

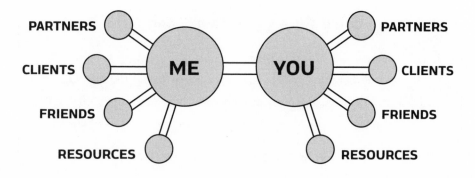

As I finished writing this chapter, I had the good fortune to meet Dave Logan, a former Associate Dean at USC's Marshall Business School and co-author of NY Times #1 bestseller, *Tribal Leadership*. Logan's book provides keys to successful tribes (social, cultural, and business). Above all tenets, the research of Logan and his partners showed that selfless collaboration for greater good is the dominant strategy of effective leaders and relationship-builders.

Trusted influencers not only introduce fellow tribe members, but members of different tribes; even strangers to strangers, expecting nothing in return. By definition, this means *anyone* can be a power networker among friends, peer groups, and global communities. Simply follow these universal laws, and you're guaranteed to be a great leader of any tribe.

10 LAWS OF HIGHLY SUCCESSFUL NETWORKERS

1 Smile.
2 Be honest and be yourself.
3 Show respect, humility, and gratitude.
4 Introduce others; even strangers you just met.
5 Ask friends and colleagues for warm introductions.
6 Ask questions. Listen intently. Find common ground.
7 Offer to help others before asking for what you want.
8 Consider everyone a potential friend, partner, or mentor.
9 Be willing to share ideas and resources - expect nothing in return.
10 Be clear about what you want, who you want to meet, then ask politely.

Bonus Rule # 11 — Think Long Term

Quality relationships take time. Make an effort to meet your host, leaders, and competitors; a partnership may be on the horizon. Take good notes when meeting someone; then follow up. E-mails are great but handwritten thank-you notes never go out of style.

When we care, they care.

Final Thoughts

> *"Lust is easy. Love is hard. Like is most important."*
> CARL REINER (1922 –)
> American Comedian, Actor, Writer, Director, Producer

> *"You can't always sit in your corner of the forest and wait for people to come to you — you have to go to them sometimes."*
> WINNIE THE POOH (1926 –)
> Fictional Bear, Created by A.A. Milne, Adapted by Disney

IN A LIFETIME, YOU'LL network with hundreds, thousands, or maybe millions of people, especially in today's world of social networks. Either way, be present in the moment, but think long term. People will come and go. We won't love everyone and not everyone will be nuts about us. So give special attention to those who deserve it most: family, friends, and quality relationships.

Be genuine and people will like you — be phony and everyone will know it.

Connect the Dots

How Relationships and Networking Connect to The 4 Essentials	
SKILLS	» Relationships teach skills and fill our gaps.
STRATEGIES	» Relationships drive teams, personal growth, and business development.
VALUES	» Relationships demand trust, respect, patience, gratitude, and humility.
PURPOSE	» Quality relationships enhance life at work, home, and around the world.

Exercises and Story Contest

1 List your top 3 strategies for networking and building relationships.
2 Write a story about a relationship that changed your life or business.

RULES AND ENTRY FORM: www.cliffmichaels.com.

Strategy 4
Decisions and Problem Solving

> *"Indecision may or may not be my problem."*
> JIMMY BUFFETT (1946 –)
> American Singer, Songwriter, Entrepreneur

Let's Go ... Decide Already!

Decisions are often driven by emotions. What if I fail? Will I feel good? What if I make the wrong choice? On the other hand, we're motivated by logic. How much will it cost? Is much effort required? Is this good for business? Better questions might be: Who's been down this road before? What worked? What didn't? What lessons were learned? Some decisions require deliberate thought. Others call for swift action. We can't always form committees and no one makes the right choice all the time. The best we can do is make the most educated choice, based on time and information at our disposal.

What Would Einstein Do?

ASK THE RIGHT QUESTION

I DID A BOOK report on Albert Einstein when I was in 8th grade. It changed my life. Einstein said, "If I had an hour to solve a problem and my life depended on it, I would use the first fifty-five minutes to formulate the right question. Once I've identified the right question, I can solve the problem in less than

151

five minutes." So in honor of my hero Albert, I've developed five questions that always start my decision-making filter.

1 What does my gut tell me?
2 What's the best, worst, or most-likely scenario?
3 Is this decision negotiable? What if ...? Can we ...? Why not ...?
4 Can I have fun and flip a coin (heads-vanilla, tails-chocolate)?
5 Can I get help or delegate the decision; then live with the outcome?

What Would Socrates or Franklin Do?

WEIGH THE PROS AND CONS

If we go back a few thousand years, we discover the Socratic Method, named after Greek philosopher, Socrates. In the process, debating parties present opposing views to stimulate intelligent ideas. We only have to trek back a few hundred years to learn a similar approach by Ben Franklin. Faced with a dilemma, Franklin would draw a line down a piece of paper — on one side he listed rewards, on the other side risks. Franklin's system is easier to illustrate.

The following is a Franklin Approach to a potential partnership. This analysis could apply to small entrepreneurs or large companies alike.

Rewards of a Merger	Risks of a Merger
• New assets & revenue	• New expenses & liabilities
• New clients	• Increased customer headaches
• New ideas & talent	• Clashing styles & personalities
• New passion & enthusiasm	• Different values & work ethic
• More experience	• Less control

A partnership is obviously more complex than a decision between vanilla and chocolate. You may have to throw pros and cons on a whiteboard or retreat to a remote cabin with your team. If there's a stalemate, it may be time to rope in objective advisors. A common mistake we've all made is trying to solve problems beyond our capacity, especially when we're emotionally or financially attached.

The Essential Questions

What's your mission? Why are you doing it? Who are you doing it with?

Cost Benefit Analysis

In the end, almost every good choice boils down to **Cost-Benefit Analysis.** But whether you're a student, parent, CEO, or globetrotter, your most difficult budget decisions will always be based on one or more of these three keys.

1 **Time:**   Is it worth the hours, months, or years?
2 **Money:** Is it worth the dollars and cents?
3 **Effort:** Is it worth the energy or aggravation?

For extra credit in real-world economics, remember this credo:

Too many chefs in the kitchen can spoil the soup,
and sometimes you need extra brains in the boardroom.

Some decisions are best handled on our own while others require teamwork. Either way, acknowledge that some things will go your way and others will fail miserably no matter how smart you plan.

Whatever you do, decide. You can't enjoy the ice cream if you never pick a flavor.

Final Thoughts

"Even if you're on the right track, you'll get run over if you just sit there."
WILL ROGERS (1879 – 1935)
Cherokee Actor, Cowboy, Humorist

WHEN MAKING DECISIONS, IT'S easy to get lost in a quagmire of emotions. Avoid the drama festival. Happy and successful people get very good at solving problems by making the process routine. Decisions are often less complicated than we make them out to be. Unless you're Steven Hawking trying to calculate a "Theory of Everything" in the known universe, odds are good that a solution to your problem exists.

If all else fails, don't forget to look it up or ask for help. And of course, the wisdom of Einstein, Franklin, and Socrates are always at your disposal.

Connect the Dots

How Decision Making and Problem Solving Connect to The 4 Essentials	
SKILLS	» Problem-solving sharpens creative skills, practice routines, and crisis management.
STRATEGIES	» Problem-solving improves negotiation abilities, teamwork, leadership, conflict resolution, and goal execution.
VALUES	» Problem solving requires patience and perseverance.
PURPOSE	» Decisions aligned with purpose are always more successful.

Exercises and Story Contest

1 List your top 3 strategies for decision making and problem solving.
2 Write a story on decisions or problem-solving, describing what worked, what failed, and your biggest lessons learned.

RULES AND ENTRY FORM: www.cliffmichaels.com.

Strategy 5
Teams, Leaders, and Advisors

> *"You're looking for players whose name on the front of the jersey is more important than the one on the back."*
> HERB BROOKS (1937 – 2003)
> American Hockey Coach, 1980 Men's Olympic Team

Teamwork

Whether you're a committee of 2 or division of 20, great teams rule the day. As a kid, my first exposure to teamwork was soccer; I played on last-place teams and championship clubs alike. Those were great learning years that taught me the importance of commitment and self-sacrifice. As an adult, I had the good fortune to work with inspirational leaders and selfless business partners, but I also saw the damage caused by ego or selfish behavior; and how either can sabotage morale and productivity. Considering the time, money, and energy saved, there's no doubt in my mind that collaboration nearly always trumps solo.

As a corollary to the above, the following Olympic flashback is my favorite reminder of why teams, not individuals, win championships.

Do You Believe?

AT THE 1980 WINTER Olympics, a squad of unknown American college kids defeated a world-class Soviet Union team in men's hockey. The victory was voted the greatest sports moment of the 20th century by *Sports Illustrated*. A made-for-television movie (*Miracle on Ice*, 1981) was also released shortly after. Hollywood couldn't write a better script. Was Team USA the most talented or experienced? Hardly. The college runts were considered no match for the mighty

Russians, a hockey team that had won the gold medal in every Olympics since 1956. The 1980 USA team were a pack of amateurs, assembled only months before the Olympics. It was boys versus men. David versus Goliath.

Not only had the Russians defeated the National Hockey League All-Stars in previous years, they manhandled Team USA by a score of 10-3 in an exhibition game two weeks before the Olympics. In early rounds of the tournament, the Americans would also be facing heavily-favored Sweden and Czechoslovakia. Team USA wasn't even expected to make the semi-finals against the Russians, let alone defeat Finland for Gold in the finals two days later. Oh, but they did ...

Team USA Coach, Herb Brooks, knew his American boys didn't measure up on skill or experience. Brooks had been a player himself on the '64 and '68 Olympic teams which failed to win any medal, let alone Gold. However, Brooks coached the University of Minnesota to three championships after taking over a losing program. Given his unique experience as player and coach, Brooks believed the Russians were overconfident. He also sensed the Americans could surprise anyone with the ultimate team system.

There would be no stars on Team USA. A Brooks squad would require self-sacrifice and a zero-tolerance policy for egos and malcontents. The team mantra was quoted for decades following the '80 Olympics:

"The name on the front of the jersey is more important than the one on the back."

I had just turned 13 during the '80 Olympics. I was a huge hockey fan, but had never heard of a single USA player. Talk about anchoring the definition of team at such an impressionable age. With the Americans leading 4-3, and moments to go in the final period against the Russians, I can still hear play-by-play announcer, Al Michaels, screaming at the top of his lungs, *"... 10 seconds ... 5 seconds ...*

... DO YOU BELIEVE IN MIRACLES? YES!!!"

1980 Winter Olympics, Men's Hockey, Lake Placid, New York

Feb 22, 1980
USA 4 – Russia 3 (Miracle victory in semi-finals)

Feb 24, 1980
USA 4 – Finland 2 (Gold medal in finals)

Amazingly, superior talent and experience (professionals) weren't enough for the Russians. Limited skills and inexperience (college amateurs) didn't hinder the Americans. The "miracle" hinged on a *team* mission (Olympic Gold), a *team* vision (sports history), and *team* values (pride, respect, commitment).

When the '80 Olympics were over, I had a new appreciation for teamwork. I realized the best team didn't always win — truly great teams understand that extra minds and muscle only work with a shared mission and value system. This is as true for sports clubs as it is for business teams. In short, the more successful we hope to be, the more collaborative we have to be.

Who Leads Your Team?

Growing up an aspiring athlete in Los Angeles, I had my pick of teams and I followed them all (USC, UCLA, Dodgers baseball, Lakers basketball, Kings hockey). I saw coaches come and go, but by the time I was eight years old, the greatest coach in sports history retired. I never met him but I did study his trademark success system as an adult. Many times when faced with challenges, I turned to this man for wisdom. He had just passed away at age 99 when I wrote this chapter. In his honor, I wanted to thank him for setting a leadership standard for athletes, coaches, and executives. He was not only a mentor for athletic performance and business excellence, but a model for winning in life.

I speak of course about Hall-of-Fame, college-basketball coach, John Wooden (1910 – 2010). He was affectionately known as the Wizard of Westwood at UCLA, a nickname he humbly rejected because he always gave credit to his players. Under his leadership, boys became men and teams became legend. Wooden was best known for his 10 NCAA championship teams in a span of just 12 years, including 7 in a row. There were 620 wins, 19 conference championships, and a home-winning streak that once spanned 98 games. Wooden's Bruins also played four undefeated 30-0 seasons, two of them back-to-back. There was even a 4-year span that included 88 consecutive wins. These accomplishments are staggering for any sport, but if you talk to players coached by Wooden, they invariably point to his team principles first and statistics second. One former Bruin was Los Angeles Laker Hall-of-Famer, Kareem Abdul-Jabbar. He won 3 NCAA Championships under Wooden before he became the NBA's all-time leading scorer, a 6-Time League MVP, and a 6-Time NBA World Champion. When asked about his greatest influences, Jabbar frequently said it was an "honor and privilege" to learn life lessons from Wooden, a man who made him a better leader, teammate, and human being.

In his bestselling book, *Pyramid for Success*, Wooden describes what he feels are the building blocks of winning. Ironically, Jabbar told Wooden he thought the pyramid was "corny" when he first saw it as a freshman. As a graduate, Jabbar later acknowledged the genius in Wooden's philosophy. Wooden's *Pyramid* included an essential set of skills, strategies, and values. They ranged from enthusiasm, practice, and teamwork to humility, patience, and self-discipline. Among his principles, he also emphasized personal character. As a result, Wooden turned players into more than basketball champions. He turned them into highly successful men.

In 2002, Wooden was given the Presidential Medal of Freedom, the same award bestowed on pioneers such as Martin Luther King, Jr., Stephen Hawking, Helen Keller, and Jonas Salk. In 2009, the *Sporting News* also listed the "50 Greatest Coaches" of all time. To no one's surprise, Wooden was #1.

So if you're looking for a leader to emulate, Wooden's name will always be synonymous with victory, grace, and excellence. On that note, here's my favorite Wooden quote:

"It's what we learn after we think we know it all that counts."

Boards - Forums - Advisors

Whether you have a kick-back lifestyle or a 24/7 globe-trotting business, it never hurts to have teammates who have *been there, done that.* So consider forming a brain trust or personal forum. Bouncing ideas off trusted peers is a great way to escape the confines of your own mind. Moreover, you don't need a business to start a support group. We all deal with challenges.

I'm also a firm believer in advisory boards. Experienced talent can be your ticket to finance, networks, and strategies. That said, boards are often over-hyped and under-used. So "never" give up company shares or voting rights to "anyone" without first creating benchmarks, timelines, and consequences. Performance matters!

For more ideas on building great teams, boards, and forums, including tools and exercises to run effective meetings, visit: www.cliffmichaels.com.

Final Thoughts

"We must all hang together, or assuredly, we shall all hang separately."
BENJAMIN FRANKLIN (1706 – 1790)
American Politician, Author, Inventor

W E EACH HAVE AN ensemble cast in life and business. The *Essential* questions are: Who's on your team? Who leads your team? Do you have a shared mission, vision, and value system? These days, teams are expanding globally. So find your common purpose and complimenary skills, then collaborate like never before!

Connect the Dots

How Teams, Leaders, and Advisors Connect to The 4 Essentials	
SKILLS	» Teams and leaders perform better by sharing skills.
STRATEGIES	» Teams and leaders save time and energy by sharing responsibilities.
VALUES	» Teams and leaders foster sportsmanship and democracy.
PURPOSE	» Teams and leaders fill gaps, allowing each member to focus on unique abilities. Teams are also more fun than flying solo.

Exercises and Story Contest

1 List your top 3 team principles. If you don't have them, take a team retreat to crystallize your mission, vision, and values.
2 Write an inspirational team story about life, sports, or business.

RULES AND ENTRY FORM: www.cliffmichaels.com.

Strategy 6
Focus and Time Management

> *"Get rid of the crappy stuff."*
> STEVE JOBS (1955 –)
> American Entrepreneur, Co-Founder of Apple Computers
>
>
> *"Besides the noble art of getting things done,*
> *there is a nobler art of leaving things undone.*
> *The wisdom of life consists in the elimination of nonessentials."*
> LIN YUTANG (1895 – 1976)
> Chinese Writer, Inventor

To Do or Not To Do ...

THERE ARE 86,400 SECONDS in a day. That's 31,536,000 seconds in a year. If those were dollars, and you had to use them or lose them, how would you spend your newfound wealth? We spend 1/4 to 1/3 of our lives in bed (assuming six to eight hours sleep). As for the other 2/3 to 3/4 of our lives, it all depends on choices.

For many of us, a good book, glass of wine, or favorite TV show are the only mission at day's end. Sorry, I can't let you off that easy — we have to factor in mystery mayhem! The real world doesn't stop for our to-do list. It rains. Computers fail. Partners disappear. Bills pile up. Stuff happens! Now we're a month behind — again!

By the way, it's not that I'm attention deficit, it's just that ...
oh look ... a dancing squirrel ... sorry ... what were we talking about?"

E-mails and social media compete for our attention. The door keeps knocking and the phone keeps ringing. We type with one hand and make calls with the other. We attempt to be a Jack-of-all-trades but we master none. How can we prioritize amid the never-ending siege to our senses? "Focus," you say? There's that squirrel again. How does he do that dance?

Let's face it — everyone's head is spinning with personal issues and intellectual interference. We're deluding ourselves if we think focus happens with a finger snap. So how do we put focus into practice?

I'm glad you asked.

The 5 Focus Rules

Assuming you can ignore dancing squirrels ...

FOCUS RULE # 1: TURN OFF THE NOISE FOR A DAY
Unplug the television. Shut off the computer. Put down the cell phone. I know what some of you are thinking. "No calls? No E-mail? No social media? That's crazy, Cliff! What will the world do without me for a day?" I assure you, life goes on. The world will happily await your glorious return.

FOCUS RULE # 2: OWN YOUR TIME / MANAGE EXPECTATIONS
Let everyone know the boundaries of your schedule. Be unavailable certain days or times. Then commit to getting things done during those focus hours.

FOCUS RULE # 3: COMMIT TO YOUR UNIQUE ABILITY
Focus on core strengths. Don't waste time perfecting weaknesses.

FOCUS RULE # 4: ELIMINATE NON-ESSENTIALS
Reduce the number of projects and meetings on your plate. Focus on "the one thing" that has the greatest impact on everything else.

FOCUS RULE # 5: SPACE MANAGEMENT
Want success? Clean up the mess! Time + Space Management = Focus

Why Do We Procrastinate?

It's hard to say which calendar system is best for scheduling tasks and appointments. It's personal. Suffice to say, we all need to write things down if we're serious about goal execution. But there's a devil in the details — procrastination is more often about psychology than checklists.

When tasks aren't getting done, it's frequently because we associate them with some degree of pain. Maybe fear of failure prevents us from giving 100%. Maybe it's something we hate to do, like studying for a test. How about avoiding the dentist because we hate needles. Perhaps the pain will just go away.

Guess what? Fears, pain, and challenges don't go away by themselves. They can multiply and get worse!

Hey — there's that squirrel again.
Is he really doing a Michael Jackson moonwalk?

In the end, we all procrastinate; not just due to fears, but sensory overload. Most of us never learned to handle major projects and challenges at the same time, let alone the guilt when a bad cycle begins. Consequently, if our plate gets even a little full, we say, "Screw it!"

Now we know the problem.

No more excuses.

Focus.

The solution is on the following page.

7-Step Plan to Kill Procrastination

1 **Write Down Goals and Clear Tasks in a Day-Timer**
   Post-it stickers and scribble notes only go so far.

2 **Categorize**
   Health, wealth, work, finance, projects, charity, playtime, education.

3 **Prioritize (Daily, weekly, monthly, short term, long term)**
   Start with the highest priorities each day.
   End each week and month scratching stuff off the list.

4 **Focus on Baby Steps**
   Tackle a little each day rather than do nothing.
   Better to do one thing now than leave ten things hanging.

5 **Delegate or Collaborate**
   Drop the ego. Ask for help. You can't do it all.

6 **Assign a Focus Friend**
   Is it time to step up accountability? Ask a buddy to kick your ass!

7 **Make it Fun and Rewarding?**
   Add music, competition, or inspirational surroundings that make
   work, play, and relationships more exciting! If you associate pleasure
   with the task you're avoiding, you'll be more likely to get it done.

Final Thoughts

"Many people take no care of their money till they come nearly to the end of it. Others do just the same with their time."
JOHANN WOLFGANG VON GOETHE (1749 – 1832)
German Writer and Polymath

FOR HIGH PERFORMANCE PEOPLE, busy calendars go with the territory. However, the more we cram into our schedule, the harder we make each task. We also create more stress. So pick your priorities with care. Bank on chaos and challenges. Every second spent on one activity is at the expense of another.

Now, let's go watch that squirrel break-dance.
The next show starts in five minutes!

Connect the Dots

How Focus and Time Management Connect to The 4 Essentials	
SKILLS	» Focus leads to expertise in specific skills, rather than weak skills in nonessential areas.
STRATEGIES	» Focus is critical to managing goals, people, and projects.
VALUES	» Focus builds character, commitment, and self-discipline.
PURPOSE	» Focus ensures time well-spent on priority people and projects.

Exercises and Story Contest

1 List your top 3 strategies for focus and time management.
2 Write a story about focus principles that changed your life or business.

RULES AND ENTRY FORM: www.cliffmichaels.com.

Strategy 7
Hardcore Goal Execution

> *"First comes thought, then organization of that thought into*
> *ideas and plans, then transformation of those plans into reality.*
> *The beginning, as you will observe, is in your imagination."*
> NAPOLEON HILL (1883 – 1970)
> American Author

MYTH: Written Goals Lead to Success
REALITY: Action, Accountability, and Alignment are Essential

Why Didn't They Call It, "Carpe Diem and Grow Rich?"

WHEN I WAS ABOUT 19, someone suggested I read Napoleon Hill's classic, *Think and Grow Rich* (1938). My candid reaction: "Isn't that the one with *the big secret?* Yikes — not another positive-thinking book!" By 19, I had swallowed every self-help book I could get my hands on — I was genuinely tired of anything resembling fluffy-talk. Nonetheless, I promised a friend I would read Hill's masterpiece. Millions of people loved it for a reason.

Impatient as always, I skimmed the introduction and got the gist — *positive thinking*. Then I finished the first chapter, took a deep breath, and had a totally different take than the famous title suggested. In fact, I think Hill was a genius in subtle ways I couldn't appreciate back then.

In 1908, a 20-something Napoleon Hill was a young journalist who landed an interview with industrialist Andrew Carnegie, one of the wealthiest men in the world. Carnegie encouraged Hill to research hundreds of successful men and women in hopes of discovering common threads for success. Over the next twenty years, Hill ended up studying everyone from Edison to Rockefeller. Carnegie believed the most common thread of these highly successful people was their mindset. Then in 1928, Hill and Carnegie co-published their findings under the title, *Laws of Success*. Ten years later, Hill published *Think and Grow Rich*, one of the all-time bestselling self-help books. In time, Hill's name became synonymous with his trademark expression, "What the mind of man can conceive and believe, it can achieve." No argument from me so far. Then I thought, "Hey, there's more here than meets the eye."

Hill's first story in *Think and Grow Rich* sets up his basic premise. He tells the tale of Edwin Barnes, a poor and uneducated man who has the gumption to hop a train and show up cold at Thomas Edison's laboratory, asking for an apprenticeship. Barnes wants to learn from the master inventor in hopes of someday working *with* Edison, not just *for* him. Well, someday comes — the Edison Dictating Machine is sitting on the shelf collecting dust. Barnes is so positive he can sell the machine, he persuades Edison to let him take it to market. Barnes ends up being so successful selling the machine, Edison grants Barnes nationwide distribution. Barnes ends up making millions.

MORAL OF THE STORY: a man with no money or education was able to **think and grow rich** by maintaining a burning desire and positive mental attitude.

My take on the Barnes story leads me to believe Hill's book should have been titled, *Carpe Diem and Grow Rich* or maybe *Just Do It and Grow Rich*. While positive-thinking is widely accepted as the secret to *Think and Grow Rich* (certainly implied by the book title), I'm convinced that Barnes' #1 success principle was being a man of action. Psychologists and fans of Hill may debate this. But what really comes first? Thought or action? Chicken or egg? Who's likely to be more successful — action-oriented people who never read a self-help book or positive-thinking couch potatoes?

In *Think and Grow Rich*, the action principles are baked right in: *make decisions, avoid procrastination, use your imagination*, and *acquire specialized knowledge*. Moreover, I'm certain Hill would agree that positive thinking isn't a light switch we flick on and off. We all have doubts. Life throws a curve now and then. It's when they're not positive that highly successful people show up. Like those days we don't feel like training or going to the office — we do it anyway and sometimes amazing things happen.

Amid my own fears and doubts, I bought my first property at 19, in part because I had desire, but in practice because I watched what successful investors were doing every day — they showed up when others didn't. They wrote all those "thank-you notes." That persistence is how they hit their goals and got the best deals. I may be quibbling over words, but action has to be as relevant as mindset.

Yes, my suggestion to change the title of an all-time bestseller was something of a rant by a silly teenager. I'm also sure *Carpe Diem and Grow Rich* was in the back of my mind on days I didn't feel like showing up.

As a corollary to the above, I really should express my appreciation to Mr. Hill. He truly was my first business mentor. Just don't get me started on Dale Carnegie's _How to Win Friends and Influence People_. Although Carnegie is another favorite mentor of mine, I still think the title of his classic should have been _How to Earn Friends and Build Trust_.

Hardcore Step 1: Take Personal Action

As discussed in the *Carpe Diem* chapter, there may be no greater life skill than simply taking action. If all we ever do is write goals and think positive, we run the risk of joining millions who have passionate ideas and few accomplishments.

What if Steven Spielberg had never taken the Universal Studios tour to explore real-world filmmaking or never spoken about his desire to be a big-time director when he met that studio executive? Would Spielberg have been signed as a 22-year-old director had he not *seized the day*?

How about poor and uneducated Mr. Barnes showing up on the doorstep of Edison's laboratory, dreaming to work *with* the master inventor? What if Barnes had never asked Edison for the rights to sell the Dictating Machine? Carpe diem crazy, huh?

Neither Spielberg nor Barnes required business plans, board meetings, or approval from friends to pursue their dreams. Sometimes it just pays to think less and do more. Yeah, that's the ticket — *Just Do It and Grow Rich*!

Hardcore Step 2: Create Accountability

So far, we've laid out 6 Action Strategies in previous chapters, ranging from self-discovery to team-building. It's all been leading to something a bit more hardcore — *accountability*. These next steps are designed to discourage you from fooling yourself (or others) when it comes to goals. Not that you would ever shirk your responsibilities, but in case you lose your appointment book or get distracted by a squirrel, we should cover all bases.

First, let's recap highlights from the self-discovery chapter ...

ACCOUNTABILITY REMINDERS

1 Discover your passion.
2 List and prioritize goals.
3 Focus on your unique ability.
4 Establish purpose, mission, and values.
5 Evaluate strengths, weaknesses, opportunities, and threats.

WHAT GETS MEASURED GETS DONE

Let's now assume we know our focus. We've set goals, evaluated strengths, and built great teams. How is it possible that we still manage to accomplish little or fail miserably? We sometimes lack self-discipline or fail to create accountability. We convince ourselves that all is fine when routines aren't working. Solution? Performance measurements! If you're serious about results, here's the rubric:

1 Assign a leader, decision maker, or focus sergeant.
2 Create assignments, benchmarks, and timelines.
3 Establish rewards and progress reports to keep people motivated.
4 Create contingencies (plan B) if things go wrong.
5 Create consequences (penalties) if people aren't doing their job.

P.S. Not all goals require these strict disciplines; but hardcore goals do.

HARDCORE INSPIRATION: CLIFF'S TOP 10 TIPS

Contrary to popular belief, there are countless incentives besides money that will inspire people to work, pursue goals, or play on your team. My top ten inspirational drivers are on the following table but beware of their killer counterpoints.

The underlying message is this:

Inspire or be inspired, but never inspire defeat.

10 Inspirational Drivers	10 Emotional Killers
• New or educational	• Old stuff
• Fun and adventurous	• Painful and boring
• Career advancement	• Dead-end job
• Winning championships	• No progress in sight
• Financially rewarding	• No financial upside
• Emotionally rewarding	• No sense of purpose
• Respect and recognition	• Disrespected and ignored
• Giving and volunteering	• No sense of contribution
• Positive environment	• Negative environment
• Being part of a team	• No sense of belonging

Equally important to setting goals is having every team member sign on to a shared mission, vision, and value system. Live signatures take accountability to another level. That's why the best players, owners, and executives demand benchmarks in their contracts. So if you're looking to create accountability, get everyone committed to their performance — in writing.

The results will amaze you!

Game On – Cliff Michaels

Mission: *Inspire, give back, and raise the bar.*

Values: *Fun • Integrity • Humility • Gratitude • Respect • Leadership • Excellence*

Commitment #1: I promise to do what I say.

Commitment #2: I'll be highly supportive of my teammates.

Commitment #3: I'll bring solutions to the table, not complaints.

Commitment #4: I'm responsible for my words and deeds.

Commitment #5: I'll play with passion, purpose, and conviction.

Hardcore Step 3: Alignment of The 4 Essentials

Once we're committed to action and accountability, hardcore goals must be in alignment with skills, strategies, values, and purpose. If any one goal is in conflict with any one of *The 4 Essentials*, odds for success are greatly diminished for all goals; including health, wealth, relationships, and happiness.

As we'll discover in *Essentials 3* and *4*, entrepreneurial thinking goes far beyond what we could ever learn in school even if we acquired our best skills and strategies in an academic environment. Anyone can apply benchmarks and timelines, then work hard and make money. Believe it or not, those are the easy parts. But millions of people who do that are often miserable and unsuccessful. Something is missing from their peak-performance playbook.

The secret truly successful people master is total alignment of values and purpose with their skills and strategies. This *total system for success* is certainly more challenging, but worth it.

Ready to put your hardcore Essentials to the test?

Final Thoughts

"Well done is better than well said."
BENJAMIN FRANKLIN (1706 – 1790)
American Politician, Author, Inventor

DA VINCI ONCE SAID, "Knowing is not enough; we must apply; willing is not enough; we must do." As we jump forward to *Essentials 3* and *4*, I suggest an even bolder philosophy: It's not enough to do — we must align skills and strategies with values and purpose — only then can we **Master Basic Abilities**.

Connect the Dots

How Hardcore Goal Execution Connects to The 4 Essentials	
SKILLS »	Hardcore goals drive us to improve skills and fill our gaps.
STRATEGIES »	Hardcore goals strengthen teamwork, leadership, and time management.
VALUES »	Hardcore goals require integrity, humility, and commitment.
PURPOSE »	Hardcore goals are blueprints to purpose in life and business.

Exercises and Story Contest

1 Prioritize top goals for health, wealth, passion, and purpose.
2 List the key steps, benchmarks, and timelines for your goals.
3 Write an inspirational story that required *hardcore* goal execution.

RULES AND ENTRY FORM: www.cliffmichaels.com.

Congratulations!

You've just concluded a second step toward a **Master's** in **Basic Abilities**.

Recap: The 7 Action Strategies

1   Self-Discovery and Team Mission

2   Emotional, Social, and Communication Intelligence

3   Relationships and Networking

4   Decision Making and Problem Solving

5   Teams, Leaders, and Advisors

6   Focus and Time Management

7   Hardcore Goal Execution

Essential 2 — Sophomore Degree

This diploma certifies that the reader of this book
has attained an honorary degree in Action Strategies.

Continue through *The 4 Essentials*
to graduate with a **Master's** in **Basic Abilities**

Essential # 3: **Core Values**

"Try not to become a man of success but rather ... a man of value."
ALBERT EINSTEIN (1879 – 1955)
German-Swiss Theoretical Physicist

What Do You Stand For?

CHARACTER IS DEFINED in many ways by different people. When no one is looking and things are difficult, what will you, your company, or community stand for?

For *The 4 Essentials* to work, skills and strategies must align with values. To that end, lessons I selected for this book are merely a guide. You can easily substitute the word truth for integrity, love for tolerance, or respect for gratitude. By any other name, use core values to guide your mission.

The values below ranked highest among successful people I admire.

CORE VALUES

1 Integrity (truth)

2 Sportsmanship (fairness)

3 Humility (learning)

4 Patience (the journey)

5 Tolerance (love)

6 Gratitude (respect)

7 Humor (fun)

Value 1
Integrity
Words and Deeds Matter

*"It's only when the tide goes out
that you learn who's been swimming naked."*
WARREN BUFFETT (1930 –)
American Industrialist, Philanthropist

Who Do You Trust?

When I started out in business, most of my early real estate deals were with agents, lawyers, and entertainers. As a negotiator, it was my job to read the poker faces. Translation: *Who's lying about strengths and weaknesses?* Do words match motivation? I soon learned that some people were very good at being something they're not (actors), and others often bluffed when they had no cards to play (agents and lawyers). In time, I got fairly good at reading people, especially someone's character. The experience of negotiating thousands of deals was a constant reminder about integrity.

I kept thinking about the power of words and deeds when it came to *The 4 Essentials*. This put integrity front and center when discussing values. Then I thought about how some people define success; often by money, power, or fame. So I thought it would be interesting to put two of the wealthiest and most influential men under the microscope. I wanted to see if their words and deeds matched their mission. To that end, I did a little homework on Bill Gates (Founder, Microsoft) and Warren Buffett (Chairman, Berkshire Hathaway).

It's important to note that I'm not impressed with billionaires per se. Some are worth emulating, others are not. I'm not a tech guy so my interest in Bill Gates was never about Microsoft. I don't buy stocks, so my interest in Warren Buffett was never about Wall Street. My fascination with these titans of industry was more about why they joined forces *after* making their respective billions. My findings are below ...

The Importance of Trust

"To give away money is an easy matter and in any man's power. But deciding who to give to ... how large ... when ... and for what purpose ... is neither in every man's power, nor an easy matter."
ARISTOTLE (384 BC – 322 BC)
Greek Philosopher

FOUNDED IN 2000, THE *Bill and Melinda Gates Foundation* donates billions of dollars to global causes. The foundation was started by Bill and his wife, Melinda, to solve everything from malaria and global poverty to shortcomings in education and science programs. Then in 2006, industrialist Warren Buffett contributed $31 billion dollars to the *Gates Foundation*. While the donation was unprecedented, I was fascinated to know why Buffett came to trust Gates with such a large percentage of his accumulated wealth. After all, you don't spend a lifetime building a $31 billion-dollar nest egg, then trust it to just anyone. Although Buffett has said he doesn't believe in dynastic wealth, such as leaving billions of dollars to his kids, it still begs a few questions. "Why Gates?" What was the #1 qualifier?

To find the answer, I turned to interviews and speeches the two men gave in a variety of public forums following their partnership. Common threads were easy to find. First and most obvious, Gates and Buffett didn't become trusted friends because of a mutual love for computers on Warren's part, or a need for financial advice on Bill's part. When asked about how the world's wealthiest men formed such a unique bond, Bill and Warren invariably discuss alignment of values and purpose. Chief among their shared values were gratitude and giving back. *The Gates Foundation* mission reads as follows:

"Guided by the belief that every life has equal value, the Foundation works to help all people lead healthy, productive lives. In developing countries, it focuses on improving people's health, giving them the chance to lift

themselves out of hunger and extreme poverty. In the United States, it seeks to ensure that all people, especially those with the fewest resources, have access to the opportunities they need to succeed in school and life."

Clearly, the Buffett-Gates alignment worked for many reasons — not the least of which were global resources, financial capacity, and a mutual mission to make a difference. However, my research showed that the biggest decision for Buffett boiled down to one core value above all others. It enabled him to size up Gates and say, "This is the guy I'm going to trust with my $31 billion dollars."

For the Buffett litmus test, I turned to a popular speech he enjoys giving to college students. Buffett likes to propose a hypothetical scenario where students could invest in 10% of a fellow classmate's career. Before making a final decision, the students are asked, "Which of three qualities they would consider most relevant to a classmate's future success?"

1 Intelligence and grades?
2 Effort and work ethic?
3 Integrity and character?

Buffett doesn't leave the students hanging too long. He proposes only one answer could logically measure future success — *integrity*. These are the same qualities driving Buffett's analysis of management teams when he invests in a company or trusts a buddy with loose change, say $31 billion dollars. He ends the lesson by suggesting that if each student built their principles on integrity first, success would be limitless. Buffett reminds students that none of us would ever invest in, or knowingly hire someone, who lacks character. Integrity must therefore be the base of our own value system if we want others to believe in us.

After concluding my research on Buffett, I turned my attention to Gates. His focus clearly went through a renaissance from early days at Microsoft, sometimes marred in antitrust lawsuits against the United States. Was Gates really the monopoly-driven mogul some people portrayed him to be? In his early years he was, perhaps, less altruistic. But in my study of Gates, I turned up a passage from a commencement speech he gave at Harvard, 35 years after dropping out. Just a few lines from the speech affirmed for me that Gates had evolved, and that Buffett made the right choice, for the right reasons, at the right time in history.

*"Taking a serious look back, I do have one big regret.
I left Harvard with no real awareness of the awful inequities in the world —
the appalling disparities of health and wealth and opportunity that condemn
millions of people the lives of despair. I learned a lot here at Harvard about
new ideas, economics, and politics. I got great exposure to the advances
being made in the sciences — but humanity's greatest advances are not in
its discoveries; but in how those discoveries are applied to reduce inequity."*

BILL GATES – HARVARD COMMENCEMENT SPEECH (2007)

After reviewing the Gates speech on inequities, I concluded that Buffett's
decision to trust *The Gates Foundation* with $31 billion dollars was essentially
based on the character of Bill and his wife, Melinda. Bill's commitment to global
philanthropy was even more evident in 2008 when he stepped down from his
day-to-day role at Microsoft. This enabled him to focus on a slightly bigger
mission — healing the world.

The Giving Pledge

In 2010, Bill, Melinda, and Warren pushed the philanthropy envelope a step
further. They issued a challenge to the wealthiest billionaires to pledge 50% of
their net worth to charities during their lifetimes or upon death. If successful,
this mission would change the face of global giving. In its first year alone, the
Giving Pledge secured signatures from 40 billionaire-philanthropists. Among
them are George Lucas, Paul Allen, Ted Turner, Michael Bloomberg, David
Rockefeller, and over a dozen billionaire couples.

These days, finding integrity in global leaders is challenging. We've all
watched the wealthiest men and women talk a good game (politicians, celebrities,
business giants), but their words and deeds don't always match.

In the end, Bill, Melinda, and Warren chose to leave the world with more
than money. They will leave behind lessons in character and giving. For me, these
lessons were so highly-connected to *The 4 Essentials*, they deserved a spotlight in
this book; a gentle reminder for each of us to give back the best we can.

Also see Essential 4, Purpose Principle 3: **Embrace The Art of Giving**

Final Thoughts

"One of the most important ways to manifest integrity is to be loyal to those who are not present. In doing so, we build the trust of those who are present."
STEPHEN COVEY (1932 –)
American Author, Corporate Trainer

L ET'S NOT PUT BILLIONAIRES on pedestals for their net worth. The most valued currency in the world isn't cash. It's integrity-based capital. It's the type of capital that can't buy stocks or bonds. It's the stock others put in us — the bond between our words and deeds. It's important to remember that trust is hard-earned and easily lost. So think of honest words and good deeds as deposits that yield both trust and respect.

The question is, "Did you make a large deposit today?"

Connect the Dots

How Integrity Connects to The 4 Essentials		
SKILLS	»	If we surround ourselves with honorable people, and exhibit character ourselves, we'll develop and attract essential skills and talented people.
STRATEGIES	»	Integrity is critical to teamwork, leadership, and relationships.
VALUES	»	Integrity develops humility, respect, and gratitude.
PURPOSE	»	A meaningful purpose in life or business begins with truth and character.

Exercises and Story Contest

1 List 3 of your mentors who embody character.
2 List 3 strategies you follow each day to practice integrity.
3 Write an inspirational story on someone who embodies character.

RULES AND ENTRY FORM: www.cliffmichaels.com.

Value 2
Sportsmanship
The Lost Art

> *"One man practicing sportsmanship*
> *is far better than fifty preaching it."*
> KNUTE ROCKNE (1888 – 1931)
> American College Football Coach, Notre Dame

Winners and Losers

At the playground, we were told to pass the ball. Be gracious when winning and just as cool if you lose. These days, we watch sports wondering, "Who are the kids and who are the adults?" Lunatic parents push to win at all costs. Professional coaches and players throw tantrums over bad calls. Hockey fans are conditioned to accept fighting as part of the game (5-minute penalty). I know, I know — tradition. Besides, we can't spoil Rodney Dangerfield's best one-liner, "I went to a fight the other night ... and a hockey game broke out!"

Did I mention the steroid era? No need to consider the damage we've done to a generation of athletes getting mixed signals. Eventually there are choices. We can cheat our way to money and fame or compete with integrity and pride. We can win with style or jam it down an opponent's throat. These days, the line is often blurred between winners and losers.

Fortunately, now and then, someone shows us the way ...

The Trip Heard 'Round the World

ON JULY 26, 2008, 5-foot-2-inch, Sara Tucholsky, smacked her first career home run in a Division 2 NCAA women's college softball game. It was the last game of the season and Game 2 of a doubleheader. The winning team would move on to play for a post season championship. Sara's three-run shot gave the Western Oregon Wolves an early second-inning lead. A backup right-fielder marred in a slump, Sara had just 3 hits in 34 at-bats all year — a meek batting average to say the least. She only started the game as a defensive replacement. The fact that this was her last game as a graduate and had just hit her first home run was a thrilling story by itself; the kind of drama usually reserved for Hollywood. But little Sara's home run wasn't the only story that day ...

Flash Back >> Two runners on ... Two out ... No score ... Bottom of the second inning ... Here's the pitch ... Tucholsky swings ... it's a long drive to left-center field ... the outfielder looks up ... it's gone! The crowd goes nuts! Did that really just happen? Little Sara? A home run?

Rounding first base, Sara misses the bag. As she turns back, her cleats jam, her body goes one way, her knee goes the other. In excruciating pain, she goes down. She's torn her anterior-cruciate ligament. Her coach screams for Sara to get back to first base. The rules don't allow teammates and coaches to help. The scene is pure chaos as two runners score and Sara crawls back to first. The umpire has never seen this before — a home run where the base runner can't complete a trip around the bases? The rule book isn't handy. The umpire instructs the coach and surrounding players that if she can't circle the bases, the hit will be a 2-run single instead of a 3-run home run. (*Turns out NCAA rules allow an injured batter or runner to be substituted, but in the heat of the moment, the umpire is unaware of the rule*).

The opposing team that day are the Wildcats of Central Washington University. One of their players is starting first baseman, Mallory Holtman, a superstar and team leader in hits and home runs. She's considered one of the greatest players in her school's history. Like Sara, Mallory is a graduating senior and this is her last shot at postseason glory. Ironically, Mallory would be facing double-knee surgery at the end of the season, a surgery she postponed to finish a run at a championship title. As the umpire scrambles for a solution to this unprecedented moment, Mallory says, "Excuse me, can I help her around the bases?" (*There's no rule against a player assisting an opposing player, only a rule against impeding another player*). The first-base umpire confers with the home-plate umpire and says, "All right, do it."

What happens next is extraordinary. Mallory gestures to teammate Liz Wallace, who along with Mallory looks upon a teary-eyed Sara, still lying on the ground in pain. "We're going to pick you up and carry you around the bases," says Mallory. Sara approves the gesture and says, "Thank you." As Mallory and Liz lift Sara above the ground and begin the trip around the bases, Mallory says, "You hit it over the fence — you deserve it." As they circle, Mallory and Liz slow down to allow Sara's foot to tap each base. "This has to look hilarious to everybody watching," says Liz. I wonder if they're laughing at us," says Mallory, as the girls share a private giggle. They arrive at home plate and pass the torch to Sara's teammates who welcome her like she's just hit the game-winning homer in a World Series. A crowd in tears roars with approval. They've just witnessed a once-in-a-lifetime moment.

By the time Sara looks up, Mallory and Liz are back on the field, gloves in hand, ready for the next play. They expected nothing for their act of kindness, knowing it could ultimately cost the Wildcats their shot at post-season glory. Although Mallory had two hits that day, and the Wildcats managed 2 runs, it wasn't enough. Sara's 3-run home run would prove to be the difference in a 4-2 victory. It was the first and last home run of her career.

In the media frenzy to follow, Mallory never considered her gesture special. She always said any of her teammates would have done the same. But how many people step up when it counts? Thankfully, the story became one of the most recognized moments in sportsmanship history. At the 2008 *ESPY Awards*, ESPN honored Sara, Mallory, and Liz with the year's *Best Moment* in sports.

Fast-Forward to 2010 >> Sara's softball career ended that fateful day when she tore up her knee. Mallory continued to play ball after college. The coolest part of the story though is that the two girls remained close friends, became motivational speakers, and started their own foundation, giving back to individuals and families who exemplify sportsmanship. The twist of fate that brought them together became a catalyst for doing an even greater good.

Take note future legends of the playing field — these girls got it right!

Final Thoughts

My Top 5 Sportsmanship Essentials

Essential 1: Respect teammates and competitors
If you want respect, show it.

Essential 2: Respect the game rules
If you don't like the rules, don't play.

Essential 3: Don't make excuses
You lost? Learn from it. Get over it. There's no crying in baseball.

Essential 4: Lead by example
Be first to show up and first to admit when you blew it.

Essential 5: Stay cool
Focus on the mission; not the madness of the moment.

Connect the Dots

How Sportsmanship Connects to The 4 Essentials	
Skills	» Sportsmanship builds character and self-discipline.
Strategies	» Sportsmanship is essential to winning teams, business relationships, and personal development.
Values	» Sportsmanship requires integrity, gratitude, and commitment.
Purpose	» Sportsmanship inspires friends, teammates, and coworkers to bring their best to the workplace and playing field.

Exercises and Story Contest

1 List 3 people who embody sportsmanship.
2 List your top 3 strategies for sportsmanship.
3 Write an inspirational story on sportsmanship.

Rules and Entry Form: www.cliffmichaels.com.

Value 3
Humility
Check Your Ego at the Door

> *"There's a difference between*
> *knowing the path and walking the path."*
> LAURENCE FISHBURNE AS MORPHEUS
> American Actor, *The Matrix*, Warner Bros. + The Wachowski Brothers (1999)

The More We Know, The Less We Know

IT'S 4:00 A.M. — I can't sleep. I've been rewriting this chapter for months. Frustrating. I have no witty story, just a serious case of writer's block. This is humbling, isn't it? Then it hits me. No one in their right mind can write about humility without first disclaiming the obvious; none of us have all the answers. So I e-mailed a few friends and said, "There's this chapter I'm writing on humility. I'm struggling here. Any ideas?" Within hours, several colleagues chimed back with a familiar phrase. It stuck in my head. "The more we know, the less we know." I like that. It even fits my theory on success principles; that we all have gaps. Within a week, a collaborative batch of e-mails forged the following strategy:

To bridge gaps, we must acknowledge what we don't know,
aren't good at, don't have time for, or don't like to do.

That's it. Humility is the mother of entrepreneurial thinking Without humility, there's no personal growth, no innovative ideas, no search for truth. It's our ability to say, "I don't know. I need help. Should I delegate, collaborate, or eliminate? Am I going beyond my emotional, intellectual, or financial budget?" After all, we can't do it all and no one masters it all. The secret is to focus on

191

strength and admit to weakness. The sooner we do, the sooner we'll fill our gaps.

Now I know what some of you are thinking – there are highly successful athletes, celebrities, and millionaires with huge egos, fame, and fortune, but zero humility. Right? True. However, the ones who lack humility alienate friends and coworkers. This often leads to wasted time and financial loss. In worst cases, arrogance leads to legal battles that wreak havoc with health and relationships.

To attract teams, talent, and resources, egos must be checked at the door.
If you're unsure where the boundaries lie, the following matrix may be helpful.

The Ego Matrix

Danger Signs		Consequence and Solution
DANGER SIGN	»	Someone thinks they know everything.
CONSEQUENCE	»	Arrogance leads to poor decisions.
SOLUTION	»	**Encourage ideas. Be willing to learn.**
DANGER SIGN	»	Someone doesn't listen well.
CONSEQUENCE	»	If we don't listen, we can't solve problems.
SOLUTION	»	**Encourage feedback. Be open to change.**
DANGER SIGN	»	Someone talks too much about themselves.
CONSEQUENCE	»	If we don't keep it humble, we alienate others.
SOLUTION	»	**Listen twice as much as speaking.**
DANGER SIGN	»	Someone doesn't share information or credit.
CONSEQUENCE	»	If we don't share, others lose motivation.
SOLUTION	»	**Teach. Inspire. Collaborate.**

Recognize the danger sign.
Appreciate the consequence.
Work on the solution.

Final Thoughts

"A 65-year-old that's still learning is young.
A 25-year-old that thinks he knows it all is too old."
JEFFREY IMMELT (1956 –)
American Chairman-CEO, General Electric

THE SOONER WE ASK for help, the faster we find solutions. We have to be willing to say, "This isn't my strength. Who can do it better? Who can teach me?" From there, access to tools, teams, money, and mentors is abundant.

Computers anyone? I'll take all the help I can get!

Connect the Dots

How Humility Connects to The 4 Essentials	
SKILLS	» Humility keeps us self-aware and self-disciplined.
STRATEGIES	» Humility is critical to teamwork, communication, relationships, self-discovery, and problem solving.
VALUES	» Humility requires patience, gratitude, integrity, tolerance, and a sense of humor; especially about oneself.
PURPOSE	» Humility attracts caring and talented people; a key to success in life or business.

Exercises and Story Contest

1 List 3 people who exemplify humility.
2 List 3 things you do every day to practice humility.
3 Write an inspirational story on humility.

RULES AND ENTRY FORM: www.cliffmichaels.com.

Value 4
Patience
A Lesson from Bugs Bunny

"Patience is the companion of wisdom."
SAINT AUGUSTINE (354 AD – 430 AD)
North African Theologian

"Little by little, one travels far."
JOHN RONALD REUEL (J.R.R) TOLKIEN (1892 – 1973)
English Writer, Poet, Professor

Warning
You may need to read this chapter slowly.

Does anyone remember that spoiled girl, Veruca Salt, from *Willy Wonka and the Chocolate Factory*? "But Daddy, I want it *nowww*!" Are we much different in our high-speed culture? Don't we all want it now? We can't afford it, but thank goodness for our trusty credit cards. We don't have time to eat, but fast food is our best friend. Money. Fame. Success ... Now! Now! Now!

Perhaps it's time to slow down Energizer bunnies.
There's a wise, old lesson for all of us.

The Tortoise and The Hare

M Y ALL-TIME FAVORITE *Bugs Bunny* episode was a spoof on the timeless tale of *The Tortoise and the Hare*, attributed to Greek philosopher, Aesop. As the original story goes, a tortoise, after being mocked by a rabbit (the hare), challenges his speedy adversary to a race. Sprinting from the start, leaving the tortoise far behind, the hare is so exhausted, he opts for a nap under a tree in the middle of the race. By the time he awakens, the tortoise has not only passed him by, he's won the race.

THE FAMOUS MORAL: Slow and steady wins the race.

In Bugs Bunny's world, we discover that Cecil Turtle always beats Bugs because Cecil has a twin turtle at the finish line. No matter what shenanigans Bugs tries to pull, Cecil always wins. So now we know Cecil and Bugs both cheat. That's not the lesson I'm sharing here, but be patient, I'll get to it.

Where was I? Oh yeah, in the cartoon, Bugs (disguised in sunglasses and a gray beard)) visits Cecil to ask the secret to his racing success. Cecil convinces Bugs that the secret to speed is his streamlined tortoise shell. Cecil also suggests that floppy rabbit ears aren't aerodynamic. Convinced he can now defeat his famous foe, Bugs equips himself with a turbocharged turtle shell and a swimmer's cap to hold back his floppy ears — he's retrofitted for that extra burst of speed (suspend disbelief — it's a cartoon).

To be even more certain of victory, Bugs hires mafia goons to beat up Cecil before he gets to the finish line. But here's the kicker — the hit squad mistakenly tackles Bugs because he looks like the turtle. Final scene? Cecil is waiting for Bugs at the finish line, wearing a rabbit's costume — Cecil wins again!

BUGS BUNNY'S EPIPHANY

1 There's no need to hire hooligans.
2 The other guy may be smarter than you.
3 Never assume victory before crossing the finish line.

If you're with me so far, there's an even bigger lesson. Cecil never had a legitimate shot at victory — he's slow by nature. No rabbit should ever lose to a tortoise. Bugs on the other hand sabotages victory because he cheats and refuses to pace himself. Silly rabbit!

Does Bugs remind you of anyone you know? Perhaps a friend with little patience? Maybe someone who wastes energy or doesn't think ahead? Well, a rabbit's life expectancy is 5 to 15 years. The Galapagos tortoise lives up to 150 years. So if you think about it, the moral to this classic fable really is:

Be patient and enjoy the ride — you'll live longer and win more races.

Patience is Practical

In addition to my take on Aesop's fable and cock-eyed analysis of Bugs and Cecil, my personal guarantee is that you'll live longer, feel sexier, and make more money exercising patience. Hear me out (or hare me out), just don't jump to conclusions on this.

If we rush, we tend to make more mistakes. While failure is part of life, screwing up due to impatience implies that we're unreliable. That's the last message we need to send when building relationships. Since I've always been a bit impatient myself (what entrepreneur isn't), I suggest four steps to improve patience. These nuggets have worked for me. I hope they work for you:

STEP # 1: STOP. BREATHE. THINK.
Consider yoga or meditation. Slowing down provides time to nourish ideas and cultivate solutions. Breathing slower also reduces impulse behavior and is good for your health.

STEP # 2: WALK BEFORE YOU RUN.
Long before an Olympic sprinter wins a 100-meter dash, she learns to crawl, stand, walk, run, and sprint – in that order.

STEP # 3: ASK FOR HELP AND WORK WITH TEAMS.
We're less effective when we try too much by ourselves. You can't do it all anyway. So whenever possible, delegate and collaborate.

STEP # 4: ENJOY THE RACE.
Slow down, Bugs Bunny. The slower we go, the more we enjoy the view.

Sometimes, it pays to be the turtle.

Final Thoughts

"A handful of patience is worth more than a bushel of brains."
DUTCH PROVERB

*"If the person you're talking to doesn't appear to be listening, be patient.
It may simply be that he has a small piece of fluff in his ear."*
WINNIE THE POOH (1926 –)
Fictional Bear, Created by A.A. Milne, Adapted by Disney

Patience provides time to gather knowledge;
Knowledge provides options and a faster route;
A faster route saves time and money;
Time and money create power and leverage;
Power and leverage lead to more opportunities;

More opportunities can lead to a happier and more successful life.

Connect the Dots

How Patience Connects to The 4 Essentials	
SKILLS	» Patience improves self-awareness, self-discipline, and social skills.
STRATEGIES	» Patience is critical to communication, negotiations, leadership, conflict resolution, and problem-solving.
VALUES	» Patience builds humility, gratitude, respect, resolve, and tolerance.
PURPOSE	» Patience allows us to see the big picture over time. If we rush through life, we'll miss the cool stuff.

Exercises and Story Contest

1 List 3 people who exemplify patience.
2 List 3 things you do every day to practice patience.
3 Write an inspirational story on patience.

RULES AND ENTRY FORM: www.cliffmichaels.com.

Value 5
Tolerance
Open Minds, Open Doors

> *"In the practice of tolerance, one's enemy is the best teacher."*
> 14TH DALAI LAMA (1935 –)
> Tibetan, Buddhist Teacher
>
> *"You have your way. I have my way.*
> *As for the right way (only way), it does not exist."*
> FRIEDRICH NIETZSCHE (1844 – 1900)
> German Philosopher

Imagine

THE FAR LEFT. THE extreme right. Shouting versus talking. I'm right, you're wrong. Are we developing a culture that promotes peace and goodwill? Do journalists and political leaders set a tone for civil debate? With ignorance and arrogance the mothers of intolerance, perhaps it's time to listen more, judge less.

Connected more than ever by social and media networks, we remain divided by race, religion, and socio-economics. We judge too quickly, often by appearance, with too much emotion, and not enough information. The results can be devastating (alienation, divided nations, loss of life).

Our social and cultural viewpoints come in part from family, media, and experience. Some are accurate, many are not. Millions of innocent people have been killed or persecuted over religion and politics (Christ, King, Kennedy). Extraordinary geniuses have been labeled crazy in their lifetime (Einstein, Mozart, Picasso). When 19 radicals hijacked airplanes and the name of Islam on September 11, 2001 (leveling New York's World Trade Center), millions of Muslims were assumed to be terrorists; the view of narrow-minded ideologues around the world.

But on October 30, 2010, at the National Mall in Washington D.C., political satirist Jon Stewart (The Daily Show), and comedic alter-ego, Stephen Colbert (The Colbert Report), did their jocular best to teach tolerance. They co-hosted a Woodstock-like event, affectionately called The Rally to Restore Sanity and/or Fear. Between two hours of witty punditry and inspirational music, the late-night TV hosts managed to deliver profound messages on a lack of civil discourse in America. Notwithstanding a musical smack-down between rebel-rocker Ozzy Osborne and '60s activist, Cat Stevens, the event highlight came in a pithy, 11-minute keynote offered by Stewart. My essential takeaway were a few brilliant lines:

"We can have animus and not be enemies. Unfortunately, one of our main tools in delineating the two broke. The country's 24-hour politico-pundit-panic conflict-o-nator did not cause our problems, but its existence makes solving them that much harder ... If we amplify everything, we hear nothing."

The irony of comedians as tolerance teachers doesn't escape me. However, it may be that Stewart and Colbert are peace ambassadors worth consideration in a cock-eyed world of amplified agendas. I'm certainly no expert on global diplomacy and claim no credentials to solve the world's problems. But if each of us has a voice in our office, church, temple, or community, perhaps we can lead by example — listen more, judge less — maybe tone it down a notch.

Our tolerance record as a human race isn't worth bragging about. So every now and then, let's remember fallen soldiers and emergency responders. Remember children and families taken too young for all the wrong reasons. Remember Dr. Martin Luther King, Rosa Parks, and Jackie Robinson. Remember spiritual leaders like Mendela, Gandhi, Christ, and The Dalai Lama. Remember the billion people who still suffer today from hunger and illness. Remember the planet we share.

One race — one soul — please remember.

Resilience and Compassion

I once hosted friends at my home to honor a Holocaust survivor named Shana. As Shana shared her story, we were all struck by the love in her voice as she recalled the most tragic of experiences. She harbored no ill will, not even toward a Nazi regime that killed millions. We were inspired by Shana's resilient and compassionate soul but were curious to how she reached such inner peace. We asked. "Why aren't you angry? How do we build tolerance among intolerant minds?" She said, "Patience. Compassion. Education. We must talk to one another. We must never forget past lessons, but live, teach, and forgive in the present."

Listening to Shana, we gained awareness of our bigger challenge in society. Parts of the world have no access to books, the Internet, or even local news. Other countries have news in abundance but are laced with political agendas and watered-down sound bites. Journalists don't always put history in context. Many citizens are ill-informed. In some cultures, public dialogue is discouraged. There are schools and communities that foster hatred. Nonetheless, we won't enlighten anyone with bombs. As Shana eloquently stated, shaping hearts and minds begins with patience, compassion, and education.

More than ever, we need tolerance without dogma.

Is Teaching Tolerance Possible?

Practically speaking, we have more to gain by engaging others for the right reasons, rather than excluding them for the wrong reasons. When we judge too quickly, we miss opportunities to meet amazing people and prosper from their wisdom; *especially* if their experience differs from our own. To that end, how is it that tolerance is not a bigger part of traditional education systems? If anyone can prove to me that math, science, and economics are more relevant than tolerance skills, I'm all ears.

Consider that intolerance isolates individuals; isolation restricts communication; when communication and teams break down, personal growth and business development suffer. I'm no math wiz, but does anyone else see the calculation conundrum?

But imagine if conflict-resolution was required learning in grade school. Imagine if tolerance principles were standard courses in high school, college, and corporate-training. Imagine if we all had to pass competency tests on values such as integrity, humility, and gratitude. As John Lennon wrote, *"Imagine."*

3 Major Benefits of Tolerance

BENEFIT # 1: HEALTH

The less we argue, the less stress on our physical and emotional well-being. If for no other reason, tolerance is a fantastic antioxidant!

BENEFIT # 2: WEALTH

The more people we get along with, the more doors we open to new friendships, social networks, and business opportunities.

BENEFIT # 3: HAPPINESS

The more lives we change through tolerance, the happier everyone will be by a factor of a million. Go ahead, look it up — I did the math.

Bonus Benefit ...

Peace & Love

Top 10 Tolerance Tips

Tip # 1:   Speak softer, not louder.

Tip # 2:   Consider dialogue over monologues.

Tip # 3:   Listen with the intention of learning.

Tip # 4:   Share ideas but don't insist on your opinion.

Tip # 5:   Make the first concession and expect nothing in return.

Tip # 6:   Turn the other cheek when intolerance is directed at you.

Tip # 7:   Don't assume you know everything from first impressions.

Tip # 8:   Leave the door open for future dialogue when you disagree.

Tip # 9:   Make a genuine effort to know someone by asking questions.

Tip # 10: Shower enemies with love, smiles, laughter ... and maybe chocolate.

Please share

Final Thoughts

"A peace is of the nature of a conquest;
for then both parties nobly are subdued, and neither party loser."
WILLIAM SHAKESPEARE (1564 – 1616)
English Poet and Playwright

IN MY WILDEST FANTASY, we would all get along. Sadly, the real world is a bit more complicated. Individuals and cultures have different views on values, religion, education, capitalism, and government. This is why our social, education, and corporate structures will never be complete without a high bar for tolerance. If this book delivers no other message, I hope this one shines through:

Listen, learn, and love — we're all just trying to chill here.

Connect the Dots

How Tolerance Connects to The 4 Essentials	
SKILLS	» Tolerance develops self-awareness and empathy for others.
STRATEGIES	» Tolerance improves communication and resolves conflict.
VALUES	» Tolerance requires patience, humility, and respect.
PURPOSE	» The more people we embrace, the more others will embrace us.

Exercises and Story Contest

1 List 3 people who exemplify tolerance.
2 List 3 things you do every day to practice tolerance.
3 Write an inspirational story on tolerance.

RULES AND ENTRY FORM: www.cliffmichaels.com.

Value 6
Gratitude
How Thankful Can We Be?

> *"Gratitude is not only the greatest of virtues,*
> *but the parent of all others."*
> CICERO (106 BC – 43 BC)
> Roman Philosopher

Gratitude 101

Consider the world we live in:

- Malaria. Cancer. AIDS.
- Thirst. Hunger. Homeless.
- Earthquakes. Tsunamis. Hurricanes.
- Physical and Emotional Challenges

Somewhere, someone is less fortunate. We have so much.
Somewhere, someone has suffered loss of life. We are alive.
Somewhere, sacrifices were made we cannot fathom. We should be grateful.

Welcome to Asia, Cliff

IN 2007, I WAS on sabbatical in Southeast Asia, searching for common threads to success and happiness. As I made my way through Malaysia, Thailand, and Singapore, I was truly struck by Asian hospitality. I had one experience however that shook me to the core. It happened my first day in Penang, a beautiful island off the Northwest coast of Malaysia.

I had just checked into my hotel and decided to go for a hike. On my trek, I came across a tiny home in the hills. A little boy and girl were chasing a chicken around a wire-fenced yard and kicking a soccer ball. I stopped to say, hello. The boy, maybe 8, didn't speak much English, but with a big smile and open arms he said, "Welcome to Malaysia. I'm Adil." He then signaled to his sister, maybe 7, and said, "This is Lily." "Well hello there, Adil and Lily. Very nice to meet you. I'm Cliff," I said with a bow. I then pointed to the chicken and jokingly asked, "What's his name?" Lily grinned and said, "Dinner. Him dinner." We all busted out laughing!

Adil then kicked his ball my way. He was shocked when I started juggling the ball on my head. I still had a few skills from my soccer days. A few minutes later, their father greeted me with a big smile, "Hello, Mr. Michaels." I recognized him as Ahmad, a staff member from my hotel. He was so grateful I had taken a few minutes to play with his kids, he invited me to dinner. I accepted the invitation, but wasn't sure if Lily's feathered friend was on the menu. Namaste, little chicken.

As it turned out, Ahmad's cousin was to be married that day with a dinner party to follow. Here I was, stranger in a strange land, being invited to a once-in-a-lifetime celebration. We arrived at a small home along a dirt road. Guests were sitting on a porch, laughing, drinking wine, playing guitar, and telling stories. Ahmad introduced me as his soccer pal from America, as if he had known me his whole life. A brief ceremony was held and dinner served. I was humbled by the warm hospitality of the bride and groom (Sarah and Kamal). I was included in each conversation and my new friends insisted I enjoy every dish as it arrived from the kitchen.

As dessert was served, Sarah and Kamal addressed everyone by name, sharing how each guest had special meaning in their lives. They expressed appreciation for a cousin's humor, sister's compassion, loyalty of close friends, sacrifice of their parents, and wisdom of their grandparents. Imagine my surprise when they finished going around the room and pointed to me. They insisted I stand up. Then they told everyone what an honor it was to make a distant traveler welcome in their home, their hearts, and their country. They said I reminded them of a family member they had recently lost, and that my visit was a well-timed blessing. Their gratitude was overwhelming. In perfect harmony, with hands pressed at heart, Sarah, Kamal, and all their guests smiled, then bowed their heads in my direction. Behind a stream of tears, I returned the bow. Then I thanked them for an evening of unconditional love and friendship I would never forget.

I had been in Malaysia less than a day. Strangers and a beautiful couple I had never met showed more love, humility, and gratitude in a few hours than dozens of opulent weddings I had experienced back home.

Life has never been the same — the bar was raised.

4 Ways to Say, "Thank You"

I left Malaysia and continued on to Thailand, the Philippines, and various parts of China. I began talking on the phone each day with friends in India, South Africa, and South America. When you see poverty and hunger at the most extreme levels, the juxtaposition of sadness and compassion are overwhelming. The word that always came to mind in travels to second and third world nations was *gratitude.*

As of 2010, there were approximately 7 billion people in the world. An estimated 925 million (1 out of 7 people) are hungry or living in poverty. That's 13% of the population.

How lucky are 87% of us?

When I returned from Asia, I made a list of people deserving of my gratitude. Below are the 4 ways I showed appreciation, depending on the relationship.

APPRECIATION STYLE # 1: VERBAL
There's no substitute for saying, "Thank you," or "I love you."

APPRECIATION STYLE # 2: PERSONAL AND VISUAL
A handwritten thank-you or custom gift basket never goes out of style. From music to framed photos, make it personal and they'll always remember.

APPRECIATION STYLE # 3: PHYSICAL AFFECTION
Gifts will never do when a hug and kiss are required. Show the love, baby!

APPRECIATION STYLE # 4: THE COMBO PACK
Knock their socks off with verbal, visual, and physical gratitude.

Final Thoughts

> *"You cannot do a kindness too soon because*
> *you never know how soon it will be too late."*
> RALPH WALDO EMERSON (1803 – 1882)
> American Poet, Philosopher

I'm thankful for failures. They teach lessons.
I'm thankful for challenges. They build character.
I'm thankful for what I don't have. It shows possibility.
I'm thankful for what I have. Too much would be a burden.

Mostly, I'm thankful for where I am. It's where I'm supposed to be.

Cliff Michaels

Connect the Dots

How Gratitude Connects to The 4 Essentials	
SKILLS	» Gratitude builds wisdom, kindness, and self-awareness.
STRATEGIES	» Gratitude improves teamwork, leadership, and relationships.
VALUES	» Gratitude requires humility, compassion, and tolerance.
PURPOSE	» Gratitude reminds us to appreciate others and what we already have.

Exercises and Story Contest

1 List 3 things (or people) you're grateful for.
2 List 3 things you do each day to practice gratitude.
3 Write an inspirational story on gratitude.

RULES AND ENTRY FORM: www.cliffmichaels.com.

Value 7
Humor
Show Me the Funny

"Don't take life too seriously. You'll never get out alive."
ELBERT HUBBARD (1856 – 1915)
American Author, Philosopher

Also famous for this quote:

BUGS BUNNY (1940 –)
Warner Brothers Cartoon Character

RYAN REYNOLDS (1976 –)
American Actor, *National Lampoon's Van Wilder*

Tickle My Giggle

IT'S A MEDICAL FACT that laughter is the ultimate cure-all for the common cold or a crappy day. Why else would we have a funny-bone? A good sense of humor also makes you happier and insanely rich — write that down. To properly examine your humor quotient, please drop your pants, turn your head, and cough; if joy and money come flying out of your butt, you're in that rare group of uniquely gifted people — good for you! For everyone else who wants to be red-hot sexier and two inches taller, it's time to show me the funny. If it makes you more comfortable, I'll show you mine first.

Thanks for coming. 2-drink minimum. Don't forget to tip your server.

Favorite Quickies

"If at first you don't succeed, sky diving is not your sport."
STEVEN WRIGHT (1955 –)
Actor, Writer, Comedian

"Those are my principles. If you don't like them, well, I have others."
GROUCHO MARX (1890 – 1977)
Actor, Comedian, Producer

"Insomnia is my greatest inspiration."
JON STEWART (1962 –)
Talk-Show Host, Author, Satirist

"Why is the man who invests all your money called a broker?"
GEORGE CARLIN (1937 – 2008)
Actor, Comedian, Author

"The trouble with the rat race is that even if you win, you're still a rat."
LILY TOMLIN (1939 –)
Actress, Comedienne, Writer

"All you need is love, but a little chocolate now and then doesn't hurt."
CHARLES M. SCHULZ (1922 – 2000)
Author, Catoonist

*"I believe there is something out there watching us.
Unfortunately, it's the government."*
WOODY ALLEN (1935 –)
Actor, Writer, Director

*"I like to crack the jokes now and again,
but it's only because I struggle with math."*
TINA FEY (1970 –)
Actress, Comedienne, Producer

"I looked up my family tree and found out I was the sap."
RODNEY DANGERFIELD (1921 – 2004)
Comedian, Actor

Favorite Quickies

"People come up with statistics to prove anything — 14% of people know that."
HOMER SIMPSON
Cartoon Character, Created by Matt Groening

"Carpe per diem. Seize the check."
ROBIN WILLIAMS (1951 –)
Actor, Comedian

"I can resist anything but temptation."
OSCAR WILDE (1854 – 1900)
Writer, Poet

"Yada. Yada. Yada."
THE CAST OF SEINFELD (153RD EPISODE, 1997)
Emmy-Winning Television Sitcom

"I base most of my fashion taste on what doesn't itch."
GILDA RADNER (1946 – 1989)
Actress, Comedienne

"Some people have a way with words ... some people ... not have way."
STEVE MARTIN (1945 –)
Actor, Comedian, Writer

"I don't know the key to success but
the key to failure is trying to please everybody."
BILL COSBY (1937 –)
Actor, Comedian, Producer

"We use 10% of our brains.
Imagine how much we could accomplish if we used the other 60%."
ELLEN DeGENERES (1958 –)
Actress, Comedienne, Talk-Show Host

"I'm just trying to make a smudge on the collective unconscious."
DAVID LETTERMAN (1947 –)
Comedian, Talk-Show Host

Final Thoughts

L EARN TO TELL AT least one joke really well. Humor is the ultimate icebreaker whether you're meeting new people or courting the object of your affection. There's a time and place for dirty jokes so be sure to know the difference if you want people to laugh with you instead of at you. As for me, my parents are from Brooklyn, New York. F-bombs were standard issue at birth so there was no profanity filter. My earliest language influences were comedic geniuses like George Carlin, Robin Williams, and Richard Pryor.

I cleaned things up for this book but in the interest of full disclosure, there's some east-coast DNA in my gene pool that I'm very proud of (spank you very much).

Connect the Dots

How Humor Connects to The 4 Essentials	
SKILLS	» Laughter is the Sugar Daddy of life and business skills.
STRATEGIES	» Humor improves leadership, communication, and relationships..
VALUES	» Humor is a sister value to fun; the key to entrepreneurial thinking.
PURPOSE	» If you laugh more, you'll be sexier, healthier, and wealthier!!!

Exercises and Story Contest

1 List your 3 favorite one-liners and commit them to memory.

2 Show Me the Funny!
   a) Make the world's funniest video.
   b) Attach a funny phrase to any photo.
   c) Write an original joke or hilarious story.

RULES AND ENTRY FORM: www.cliffmichaels.com.

Congratulations!

You've just concluded a third step toward a **Master's** in **Basic Abilities**.

Reminder

Substitute or add your favorite values.
Be sure to share them with your team.

RECAP: THE 7 CORE VALUES

1 Integrity (truth)

2 Sportsmanship (fairness)

3 Humility (learning)

4 Patience (the journey)

5 Tolerance (love)

6 Gratitude (respect)

7 Humor (fun)

Essential 3 — Junior Degree

This diploma certifies that the reader of this book
has attained an honorary degree in Core Values.

Continue through *The 4 Essentials*
to graduate with a **Master's** in **Basic Abilities**

Essential # 4: **Purpose Principles**

"I believe the choice to be excellent begins with aligning your thoughts and words with the intention to require more from yourself."
Oprah Winfrey (1954 –)
American Talk-Show Host, Entrepreneur, Philanthropist

CLICHÉ AS IT MAY sound, each of us has a mission to discover who we are, what we want, why we want it, and what we stand for. So we conclude with a simple premise in *Essential 4* — success and happiness come easier, and are infinitely more fun, when aligned with purpose.

For complete harmony of your 4 Essentials, Master these Basic Abilities. They are keys to the entrepreneurial mind of highly successful people.

THE 4 PURPOSE PRINCIPLES

1 Live Your Passion — Mind, Body, and Soul

2 Master the Health-to-Wealth Formula

3 Embrace the Art of Giving

4 Enjoy the Journey

Art

Health & Happiness

Mind, Body, Soul

The Moment

The Fun Factor

Giving

ADVENTURE

Friends & Family

Passion & PURPOSE

Purpose 1
Live Your Passion

> *"Twenty years from now you will be more disappointed*
> *by the things you didn't do than by the ones you did do.*
> *So throw off the bowlines. Sail away from the safe harbor.*
> *Catch the trade winds in your sails. Explore. Dream. Discover."*
> MARK TWAIN (1835 – 1910)
> American Author, Humorist

Be a Kid Again

AS ADULTS, WE GET busy with careers, calendars, and responsibilities. We don't intend to sell our souls, but we've all rented them in the midst of life's hustle and bustle. As kids however, we always found time to dream and play.

When I was a kid, I couldn't get enough sports, books, or movies. Then I hit the business world at 18 and obsessed about work all too often. I occasionally forgot to play. Fortunately, writing about *The 4 Essentials* got me back in touch with my inner Peter Pan. I kept asking, "Where's my next adventure — what cool thing can I do today?" It was impossible to write about inspirational ideas and not fill my calendar with stuff I loved. I soon loaded my i-Pod® with favorite tunes for morning hikes. I dedicated more time for yoga, friends, and people who mattered. I kicked off each day with an inspirational quote at sunrise and a good laugh at sunset.

For me, writing and sharing ideas with anyone who wants to improve their life is a passion. If I'm laughing, learning, and playing with people I love, it's fuel for my mind, body, and soul. So humor me. Take off your adult hat for a minute. Then put on a goofy smile and stick out your tongue. Be that kid who dreams and plays. Rediscover your biggest passion in a whole new way! If it helps, I'll even take you on a trip to my yoga class in the next essay. I have a unique story to share with a timeless lesson about breathing deep.

Up Puppy, Down Puppy

We often line up 30 minutes before Vinnie Marino's class to ensure a spot at Yoga Works in Santa Monica, California. As 80 students prepare for one of the hardest yoga experiences in town, restless energy and chatter bounce off the walls. "Not your typical serenity-now class, is it?" says a newbie. "Not quite," smiles a devoted fan. It's more like a healthy temple for hardcore yogis, looking to sweat and catch a moment of Zen."

They come far and wide for *Vinnie Mania*, a challenging blend of music-infused vinyasa, ashtanga, and Iyengar yoga. Students have even included celebrities from David Duchovny and Robert Downey, Jr. to Heather Graham and Kate Hudson.

"Let's get started. Take child's pose," says Vinnie. The room goes silent. Vinnie reminds everyone to "Block out distractions, settle in, and breathe deep." He starts with light stretches to focus inward. Within minutes, intense flow begins with a series of Warrior, Down Dog, and classic poses. Then Vinnie cranks up the tunes. This is definitely not grandma's yoga. He plays everything from acoustic and alternative to Coldplay and the Rolling Stones. It just depends on Vinnie's vibe.

For 90 minutes, Vinnie will challenge mind, body, and soul with gentle reminders on proper form and self-awareness. The class is intense and students will finish dripping wet. Like most yoga classes, we end with a little savasana (nap-time for yogis). It's an addicting workout, but Vinnie's high-performance classes and sage advice are only half the reason for his loyal following ...

An Italian-American, Vinnie grew up in New York. At an early age, he developed a passion for yoga, watching classes on TV. Drawn to meditation and spiritual authors, Vinnie convinced his parents to enroll him in a progressive high school, one that fostered alternative gym classes like yoga. It was the '70s, so Vinnie was also influenced by a drug culture and hippie generation in search of enlightenment. As a result, substance abuse started in his early teens. His yoga practice soon waned as drug exploration intensified. It was a way to feel open and free, but for a spiritual soul like Vinnie, drugs were a dead-end way of life. Fortunately, Vinnie found sobriety by his mid-20s and continued his search for something more; a greater passion and purpose.

In his youth, Vinnie's yoga practice was traditional. No one was teaching hardcore yoga while listening to classic rock 'n' roll. However, a move to Los Angeles in the early '90s reconnected Vinnie with an intense yoga practice. There was music, spirituality, and a physical challenge that reawakened his passion for personal growth. Vinnie was now high on his true drug of choice — yoga.

Serendipity soon played a hand as Vinnie became an assistant to Hall-of-Fame rock 'n' roller, Grace Slick, lead singer of Jefferson Airplane. The music legend was so impressed with Vinnie's east-coast spirit, she encouraged him to build a career around yoga. What Vinnie created next was a unique experience that combined cool music, non-judgmental wisdom, and intense yoga flow. Part of what makes a Vinnie class so much fun is that no two classes are alike. The soft-spoken but humorous New Yorker keeps things fresh with a variety of artists, lyrics, and rhythms.

Students who can't get enough of Vinnie's classes are forever grateful that a '70s kid from New York shares his passion each day for a healthy mind, body, and soul. His story personifies the magic in doing what you truly love.

~ namaste ~

Cliff's Yoga Journal

I've been taking Vinnie's classes for many years now, but I remember those first months like yesterday. A girlfriend thought I would enjoy a challenging workout. I initially thought yoga would be boring. I soon found out what Vinnie's 90-minute mania was all about. I could barely survive the first hour. Fortunately, Vinnie always reminded me to breathe. It was a few months before I listened, maybe a few years before I understood. Like all new yogis, I had to learn the difference between breathing and breathing deep.

Your turn > Breathe deep ... Hold it ... Now, let it go ...

Ahhhhhhhhhhhhhhhhhhhh.

Final Thoughts

YOU MIGHT BE THINKING, how could I write a chapter on passion and not talk about long, slow, deep, soft, wet kisses that last three days (*Bull Durham*)? Well, I'm no Danielle Steele novelist (as far as you know) so I won't be writing a love scene for Fabio and Francesca. Perhaps we'll give that a shot in a sequel book — *The 4 Essentials of Caribbean Kisses*. But here's a little passion trick for all my single and married friends alike (coming from me, a single guy when I wrote this). You know the tingle factor you get when someone makes your pulse race? Maybe it's a art, poetry, or music that makes your day? Prioritize those people, words, images, and music into your daily routine. Those constant reminders are your VIP pass to a passionate life.

If that doesn't work, hug a stranger or smile like you have a secret. Others may just reach out for a touch of your mojo.

Connect the Dots

How Passion Connects to The 4 Essentials	
SKILLS	» Passion drives us to **Master Basic Abilities**. The sooner we pursue our passions, the sooner we'll hit peak performance in life and business.
STRATEGIES	» Passion drives goals, teams, and relationships.
VALUES	» Passion drives love, commitment, and the pursuit of happiness.
PURPOSE	» Passion fuels purpose and motivates everyone around us.

Exercises and Story Contest

1 List your top 3 passions ... what gives you the tingle factor?
2 Commit time to your #1 passion every day!
3 Write an inspirational story that ties passion to success and happiness.

RULES AND ENTRY FORM: www.cliffmichaels.com.

Purpose 2
Master Your
Personal Health Formula

*"Of course I exercise — I push my luck,
run my mouth, and jump to conclusions."*
ANONYMOUS

Mind, Body, Soul

THERE'S NOTHING MORE IMPORTANT than health but we sometimes neglect the connection between our mind, body, and
soul. Fear not; no ten-pound book here! Just a few simple reminders.

For the record, I'm not a fitness expert. However, I've studied nutrition
and peak-performance athletes most of my life. I played soccer growing up
and still love cross-training between the gym, yoga, and outdoor sports. That
said, no one has to train like an Olympian to lead a healthy life. Keep in mind,
everyone has a unique body, mind, and medical history. Injuries or physical
limitations will factor in so there's no such thing as a one-size-fits-all formula.

For all the fitness gurus who care to debate the perfect diet, lifestyle, or workout routine, knock your socks off. Personal experience leads me to believe five
health systems are highly connected.

Disclaimer: *Please consult your mother, doctor, neighbor, or favorite talk-show
host before making any radical changes.*

System 1: Maintain a Healthy Mind

My father is a psychiatrist and neurologist. I'm certain my interest in how the brain works was initially fueled by a little *Pop Psychology*. Get it? But seriously, a healthy brain routine is essential for longevity, solid memory, and cognitive endurance. What we eat, see, hear, touch, or smell affects our ability to think. Thinking ability is tied to our physical well-being. The good news is anyone can tilt the health-to-wealth formula in their favor with a little brain exercise.

MY TOP 5 BRAIN ESSENTIALS

1 Read or write something each day.
2 Listen to music or play an instrument.
3 Meditate. A quiet mind is a learning mind.
4 Play memory games like chess, poker, or puzzles.
5 Chat with friends, peers, and strangers about something new.

System 2: Develop a Fitness Routine

Whether your passion is yoga, sports, or cross-training, the key is breathing and moving. In study after study, physical fitness is as critical to longevity (and a healthy brain) as anything else. Even if you have injuries or limitations, do what you can — breathe, walk, stretch, meditate — it all counts.

MY TOP 5 FITNESS ESSENTIALS

1 Enjoy favorite sports with friends and peers.
2 Go beyond your comfort zone and mix up routines.
3 Stretch or practice yoga, even 15-20 minutes per day at home.
4 Exercise, walk, or hike outdoors. Fresh air does a body good.
5 Get in 30 to 60 minutes of cardio or cross-training 3 to 5 days per week.

System 3: Master Basic Nutrition

Michael Phelps returned from the 2008 Beijing Summer Olympics with 8 Gold medals around his neck, but when news of the champion swimmer's diet hit the press, a shock wave rippled across the nutrition world. At the peak of training, Phelps was said to be wolfing down 10-12,000 calories per day just to keep weight on. Hello there, pizza and pancakes! Obviously, Phelps burned those calories through rigorous fitness routines. If you're 23 and training to be the world's greatest swimmer, you might get away with a few extra carbs and calories. For the rest of us, a smart balance is essential.

MY TOP 5 NUTRITION TIPS

1 Eat fruits and veggies rich in antioxidants.
2 Drink plenty of water (6 to 8 glasses per day).
3 Learn to balance fats, proteins, and carbohydrates.
4 Eat smaller portions and frequent meals for healthier metabolism.
5 Moderate or eliminate excess salt, sugar, sodas, alcohol, and caffeine.

System 4: Recognize the Sleep Factor

Sleep disorders are common and there are many causes. As an occasional travel junkie, recovering workaholic, and once-in-a-blue-moon insomniac, here's what I know for sure — whether you're partying like a rock star or laboring monster hours at midnight, when your body screams for rest, listen up!

MY TOP 5 SLEEP TIPS

1 Avoid sugar and caffeine close to bedtime.
2 Between 6 to 8 hours is ideal for a good night's sleep.
3 Sex and workout routines affect sleep. Have fun experimenting.
4 Don't sleep with your digital love-child. Cell phones keep you awake.
5 Avoid bright lights close to bedtime (especially computers or television).

System 5: Reduce the Stress Factor

Be it work, health, or daily chaos, stress creeps into our lives. The good news is that we're resilient by nature. The bad news is we weren't built for around-the-clock performance. My motto? Work hard, play hard, then chill out. If we push too hard, the mind and body will literally say, "Screw this!" An unhealthy routine can manifest in panic attacks, heart problems, even mental illness. Sadly, people die every day of stress-related causes in their 30s, 40s, and 50s. No amount of success is worth it. So do your best to connect the 5 health systems.

Don't forget to check with your health and wealth guru — I could be wrong.

Final Thoughts

"Be careful of reading health books. You may die of a misprint."
MARK TWAIN (1835 – 1910)
American Author, Humorist

The health-to-wealth formula is simple:

A healthy mind + body + soul = more energy
More energy = high performance
High performance = greater peace + happiness
Greater peace + happiness = true wealth

Enjoy the new math. I tutor Wednesdays.

Connect the Dots

How Health Principles Connect to The 4 Essentials	
SKILLS	» A healthy mind and body affect our ability to learn, think, and grow.
STRATEGIES	» A healthy mind and body improve focus, relationships, and decision making.
VALUES	» A healthy mind and body stem from patience, humility, and gratitude.
PURPOSE	» A healthy mind, body, and soul enable us to enjoy a longer, happier, and more prosperous journey with people we love.

Exercises and Story Contest

1 List your top 3 strategies for a healthy mind, body, and soul.
2 Write a story connecting health strategies to success and happiness.

RULES AND ENTRY FORM: www.cliffmichaels.com.

Purpose 3
Embrace The Art of Giving

"You give but little when you give of your possessions.
It is when you give of yourself that you truly give."
KAHLIL GIBRAN (1883 – 1931)
Lebanese-American Poet, Artist

"I've learned that you shouldn't go through life
with a catcher's mitt on both hands.
You need to be able to throw something back."
MAYA ANGELOU (1928 –)
American Poet, Historian, Activist

"Idealism detached from action is just a dream.
Idealism allied with pragmatism,
and rolling up your sleeves to make the world bend a bit,
is very exciting, very real, and very strong."
BONO (1960 –)
Irish Singer, Musician, Humanitarian

Question: What do these people have in common: You, Me, Oprah, Bono, Angelina Jolie, Lance Armstrong, Bill Clinton, Warren Buffett, Bill and Melinda Gates?

Answer: The ability to make a difference, each in our unique way.

The Key: We don't have to be famous or wealthy to help. The common threads to giving back are two, simple principles: *compassion* and *contribution*.

COMPASSION

One of the most essential human emotions is compassion; our ability to empathize with others — a state of mind that says, "We care."

CONTRIBUTION

Where compassion says, "We care," contribution says, "We act." What is it that each of us can do to improve the human condition?

THE BENEFITS OF GIVING

Giving back can be the difference between hope or despair, education or illiteracy, prosperity or poverty, health or illness, and life or death.

WAYS TO MAKE A DIFFERENCE

Volunteer. Mentor youth. Donate your time, money, or resources. Giving back can take so many forms, half the joy is deciding where to contribute.

The question isn't whether we can be caring citizens.
The question is how innovative or courageous our giving will be?

One for One Giving

"With every pair of shoes you purchase,
TOMS will give a pair of shoes to a child in need."
BLAKE MYCOSKIE (1976 –)
Founder, Chief Shoe Giver, TOMS Shoes

WALKING IS OFTEN THE primary mode of transportation in developing countries. Most children in such countries grow up barefoot. At play, doing chores, or just getting around, these children are at risk. Children walk for miles to get food, water, shelter, and medical help. Wearing shoes literally enables them to walk distances that aren't possible when barefoot. Shoes also prevent feet from getting cuts and sores from unsafe roads and contaminated soil.

A leading cause of disease in developing countries is soil-transmitted parasites that penetrate the skin through open sores. Wearing shoes can prevent this and the risk of amputation. Many times children can't attend school barefoot because shoes are a required part of their uniform. If they don't have shoes, they don't go to school. If they don't receive an education, they don't have the opportunity to realize their potential. There is one simple solution — *Shoes*.

In 2006, American traveler, Blake Mycoskie, befriended children in Argentina and found they had no shoes to protect their feet. Wanting to help, he created TOMS Shoes (short for Tomorrow's Shoes). Ironically, Blake had no background in shoe design. What he did have was an entrepreneur's vision with a philanthropic heart. Blake decided he would match every pair of shoes bought by a customer with a pair of new shoes for a child in need. When Blake first returned to Argentina with a group of family, friends, and staff, he delivered 10,000 pairs of shoes.

Blake's style of giving not only skyrocketed his business, TOMS revolutionized the way consumers shop. By 2010, the *One-for-One Business Model* had encouraged conscientious consumers to purchase from TOMS, generating more than 1,000,000 pairs of new shoes for children in need. In February 2009, at the Clinton Global Initiative University, former President Clinton introduced Blake as "one of the most interesting entrepreneurs I've ever met." Later that year, Secretary of State, Hillary Clinton presented Blake with the 2009 Award for Corporate Excellence, celebrating TOMS commitment to corporate responsibility, innovation, and democratic values.

Starting with just a few interns on a shoestring budget (pun intended), Blake became a shining example of what social entrepreneurship is all about. Imagine if every business had a "one-for-one" component. Young entrepreneurs and global companies alike could embark on a more humanitarian profit model, one that includes giving as much as selling.

Special Acknowledgment: Before finishing *The 4 Essentials*, a colleague introduced me to Blake. He's since written an inspirational bestseller, *Start Something that Matters.* I highly recommend it to artists, humanitarians, and entrepreneurs alike. It occurred to me that Blake's business model could easily be embraced by anyone. In that spirit, I've challenge peers to find their One for One — to live and give the best they can. As for CliffMichaels.com, I've launched a Giving Back Mission — with every sale, we provide free books, courses, and helping funds to students and global causes — one for one.

Thanks for the inspiration, Blake!

The Last Dropout

IN 1957, 17-YEAR-OLD BILL Milliken seemed to have a good life. He grew up in a middle-class suburb of Pittsburgh with the local country club at his disposal. His home life however was dysfunctional and he hated school. As a teenager, he thought he was dumb because he was thrown into a special class for slow learners. Turns out he had a learning disability but didn't realize it until adulthood. With a D-average, his self-esteem waned and he was kicked out of school. Bill started hanging out in communities he knew best; streets and pool halls. Fortunately, a chance meeting with a community leader changed Bill's life. For the first time, someone cared enough to show Bill a better way. Feeling his life was being wasted, Bill soon volunteered at a youth organization committed to troubled teens. His real-world experience with gangs, addicts, and dropouts led him to believe he could develop a solution to help others like him.

With little more than a small idea and a big heart, Bill ultimately created street academies for young people who had dropped out of school but wanted a second chance at education. He even developed live-in programs for youth and substance abusers in need of shelter and support. It wasn't long before Bill had repositioned community resources by encouraging local professionals to mentor, give back, and get involved in schools. By 1977, Cities in Schools was born. Today, Bill's nationwide organization is known as Communities In Schools (CIS).

Bill's 5-point philosophy is that every young person needs and deserves:

1 A safe place to learn and grow
2 A marketable skill after graduation
3 A healthy start and healthy future
4 A one-on-one relationship with a caring adult
5 A chance to give back to peers and communities

In writing *The 4 Essentials*, I had the good fortune to meet Bill Milliken so I ended up supporting CIS. His mission is simple: *prevent dropouts*. Whether it's eyeglasses, tutoring, or providing a safe after-school environment, when basic needs are met, students can focus. If they focus, they tend to stay in school and prepare for life. By 2010, CIS had influenced more than 1.5 million students in over 3,400 schools nationwide. Nearly 53,000 volunteers had donated over 3 million hours. The results? Approximately 80% improved attendance and performance, 78% eligible seniors graduated, nearly 90% fewer discipline incidents, and of course, *fewer dropouts!*

From a college dropout with a learning challenge, to a transformer in education systems, Bill is in a philanthropic class by himself. For nearly 50 years, Bill's commitment to youth education has been extraordinary. He served three U.S. presidents and received the *Champion for Children Award* from the American Association of School Administrators. His book, *The Last Dropout*, has been praised by everyone from U.S. Presidents to Russell Simmons (Founder, Def Jam Music), and spiritual author, Deepak Chopra.

When I met Bill, I was so touched by his humility, sense of gratitude, and simple philosophy, I thought, here's a guy dedicated to helping millions of kids. What if each of us made just a small commitment each week or once per month — to simply mentor youth, volunteer for a cause, or give back to those less fortunate?

Seriously, what if?

Final Thoughts

*"We cannot live only for ourselves. A thousand fibers connect us
... and among those fibers, as sympathetic threads,
our actions run as causes, and they come back to us as effects."*
HERMAN MELVILLE (1819 – 1891)
American Novelist

M OST OF US ARE luckier than we'll ever know. For some, our biggest worry is which pair of shoes to wear or what to eat for breakfast. In many parts of the world, people don't have such luxuries. As global citizens and social entrepreneurs, we must consider that:

- Kids are at risk.
- Over a billion people are ill, hungry, thirsty, and homeless.
- There are communities without schools and schools without books.

Someone, somewhere is suffering more than us.
What will our contribution be?

Connect the Dots

How Giving Back Connects to The 4 Essentials	
SKILLS	» Giving back builds awareness of the human condition. This attracts caring people with skills to learn from.
STRATEGIES	» Giving back expands the quality of teams, networks, and relationships. As leaders, we set the best example when we give and share.
VALUES	» Giving back requires humility, gratitude, and compassion.
PURPOSE	» Giving back not only affects the lives we touch, there are health benefits to our own mind, body, and soul ... so give as big as you can!

Exercises and Story Contest

1. List your 3 favorite causes in the world. Give a little bit today.
2. Write an inspirational story on giving back.

RULES AND ENTRY FORM: www.cliffmichaels.com.

Purpose 4
Enjoy the Journey

*"Life moves pretty fast. If you don't stop and look
around once in a while, you could miss it."*
MATTHEW BRODERICK AS FERRIS
Ferris Bueller's Day Off (1986) a John Hughes Film

Why Do We Do What We Do?

WE ALL MAKE SACRIFICES. The work hours can be brutal. But none of us wants to look back in 10 to 20 years and say, "I wish I had paid attention to the little things — I could have spent more time with people who mattered." Sure, it's easy to get distracted, but there comes a point when attempting to do it all might cause us to miss it all.

Never forget to be present in the moment.
In a whisper, it may be gone.

The Moment

- Love
- A kiss
- A sunset
- Kind words
- Celebrations
- A brilliant idea
- The punch line
- The smell of roses
- Friends and family
- The lemonade stand
- The bottom of the ninth
- The book with a torn cover
- Art, music, magic, and mystery
- The beginning, middle, and end

Don't Miss It!

The Fun Factor

"The question isn't what are we going to do.
The question is, what aren't we going to do?"
MATTHEW BRODERICK AS FERRIS
Ferris Bueller's Day Off, (1986) a John Hughes Film

20 Super Fun Things To Do

1. Start a rock 'n' roll band!
2. Host a pool or beach party.
3. Trade photos with friends online.
4. Gather troops for tv-comedy-movie night.
5. Meet and greet new people at social mixers.
6. Do something wild you've never done before!
7. Hit the town with friends at a favorite hot spot.
8. Surprise someone ... imagination has no boundaries.
9. Celebrate whatever and whenever the mood strikes!
10. Trade tunes, see a concert, and dance the night away.
11. Volunteer ... and get others involved for a good cause.
12. Get your weekend warrior groove on ... hike, surf, ski.
13. Have everyone bring something yummy to a food party!
14. Be a kid again at carnivals, theme parks, or a petting zoo.
15. Catch a little culture at your local museum or live theater.
16. Plan an annual tournament ... poker, scrabble, board games.
17. Have a Happy Festivus, Kwanzaa, Christmas, or Chanukah!
18. Attend outdoor events ... fun stuff + fun people = good times!
19. Gather a thinking group to chat about art, books, or current events.
20. Take a vacation. See the world. Expand your adventurous horizons!!!

... or just get naked!

Are We Having Fun Yet?

Final Thoughts on Your Journey

> *"Life is what happens while you're busy making other plans."*
> JOHN LENNON (1940 – 1980)
> British Singer, Songwriter, Peace Activist

THE BEST ADVICE I ever got was to enjoy the ride, laugh from the belly, and learn something new each day. From there, love what you do and who you do it with. Mostly, have fun, give back, and live with passion and gratitude.

When in doubt, chill out. The answers will come.

... or as The Beatles would sing, "Let it be."

... or as jazz vocalist, Bobby McFerrin would say, "Don't worry. Be happy."

Connect the Dots

How the Journey Connects to The 4 Essentials	
SKILLS	» Make it fun to **Master Basic Abilities**.
STRATEGIES	» The journey is simpler with proven strategies.
VALUES	» The journey is where we explore core values. Practice values in this book and add your favorites for the ultimate success formula.
PURPOSE	» Love. Health. Family. Friends. Giving back. Happiness! *Why else would success matter?*

Exercises and Story Contest

1 List your greatest moments in life.
2 Make your bucket list — stuff you still to crave to do.
3 Write a story about a journey that might inspire others.

RULES AND ENTRY FORM: www.cliffmichaels.com.

Congratulations!

You've just concluded your final step toward a **Master's** in **Basic Abilities**.

RECAP: THE 4 PURPOSE PRINCIPLES

1 Live Your Passion — Mind, Body, Soul

2 Master the Health-to-Wealth Formula

3 Embrace the Art of Giving

4 Enjoy the Journey

Essential 4 — Senior Degree

This diploma certifies that the reader of this book
has attained an honorary degree in Purpose Principles.

Congratulations! You are now a graduate of
The 4 Essentials with a **Master's** in **Basic Abilities**

EPILOGUE

Final Thoughts
to Connect the Dots

BASEBALL LEGEND, YOGI BERRA said, "90% of the game is 50% mental." Actor, Woody Allen said, "80% of success is showing up." Since I'm lousy at math, who am I to quarrel with Yogi and Woody? For what it's worth, the happiest and most successful people I've met are not celebrities or billionaires who measure wealth by fame and fortune. They measure wealth by love, purpose, and good health. They measure riches by what they're able to share with friends and family, even strangers. For me, abundance is measured by all these things and more.

In my 20's, I often failed to get my ego out of the way. I was content to be a perfectionist; often to my detriment. My passion often exposed my weakness, a lack of purpose. In my 30's, I began surrounding myself with smarter, more experienced people than ever. I gave up some control. I focused and stopped to breathe a little, one of the best strategies I know.

Overall, I didn't do too bad for a semi-dyslexic entrepreneur who failed at least once at everything he ever tried. I just remembered to keep asking, "What if?" Somehow, that little nugget keeps getting me closer to true success.

Congratulations! You're now a graduate of *The 4 Essentials*.

Here's to your amazing journey.

Cliff Michaels

Summary: Bridging The Education Gap

My goal in writing this book was to inspire, give back, and raise the bar for personal growth, entrepreneurial thinking, and global education. As for the great debate about gaps in traditional classrooms, no single success principle is exclusive to another — many are highly connected. For that matter, a professional degree is no more a proxy for success than "secrets" claimed by self-help gurus. I welcome challenges to my own theories.

Notwithstanding the above, those who graduate with a college degree are likely to earn far more in their lifetime than those who don't. End of debate. Academic environments are uniquely structured for disciplined learning and the exchange of ideas. Moreover, they provide unique opportunities to forge career networks and lifetime friendships. For students reading this book, take advantage of the opportunity if you have it. I wish I had embraced my college experience far more than I did.

Having said that, there are happy and highly successful people who never graduated from college; be it grades, choices, or challenges that steered them on a different path. So for anyone concerned that a degree defines who you are, or the permanent direction of your life, the following pages are worth a glance.

You just may recognize a few of the misfits ...

The Billionaires

No College Degree to Start Career

"I'm Harvard's most successful dropout ... I guess that makes me valedictorian of my own special class. I did the best of everyone who failed."
Bill Gates
Founder, Microsoft, From his Harvard Commencement Speech, 33 years after dropping out

Misfit's Name	Professional Claim to Fame
Bill Gates	Co-Founder, Microsoft
Paul Allen	Co-Founder, Microsoft
Steve Jobs	Co-Founder, Apple
John D. Rockefeller	Founder, Standard Oil
Mark Zuckerberg	Founder, Facebook
Ted Turner	Founder, CNN, Media Mogul
Richard Branson	Founder, Virgin Group
Andrew Carnegie	Industrialist / Philanthropist
David Geffen	Co-Founder, Dream Works
Larry Ellison	Founder, Oracle
Jack Taylor	Enterprise Rent-a-Car
William Hanna	Hanna-Barbera Cartoons
Michael Dell	Founder, Dell Computers
Hiroshi Yamauchi	Nintendo Corporation
Walt Disney	Founder, Disney Films, Disneyland
Mary Kay Ash	Founder, Mary Kay Cosmetics
Milton Hershey	Founder, Hershey's Chocolate
Ralph Lauren	Founder, Ralph Lauren Fashion

Entertainment Moguls

No College Degree to Start Career

Misfit's Name	Professional Claim to Fame
Lucille Ball	Emmy-Winning Actor, Comedian
Will Smith	Award-Winning Actor, Producer, Singer
Steven Spielberg	Oscar-Winning Director, Producer
Whoopi Goldberg	Oscar-Winning Actress, Comedienne
Woody Allen	Oscar-Winning Actor, Director, Producer
James Cameron	Oscar-Winning Director, Producer
Robert De Niro	Oscar-Winning Actor, Producer
Tom Cruise	Award-Winning Actor, Producer
Dustin Hoffman	Oscar-Winning Actor
Tom Hanks	Oscar-Winning Actor
Matt Damon	Oscar-Winning Screenwriter, Actor
George Clooney	Oscar-Winning Actor, Director
Anjelina Jolie	Oscar-Winning Actress
Sean Connery	Oscar Winning Actor
Halle Barry	Oscar-Winning Actress
Charlie Chaplin	Actor, Comedian, Director
Ellen DeGeneres	Actress, Comedian, Talk Show Host
Sammy Davis Jr.	Actor, Comedian, Singer, Dancer
Ray Charles	Grammy-Winning Recording Artist
Steve Martin	Actor, Comedian, Writer, Producer
Carol Burnett	Emmy-Winning Actress, Comedian
Brad Pitt	Actor, Humanitarian
Kevin Bacon	Actor, Six Degrees of Separation
Jamie Foxx	Oscar-Winning Actor, Comedian, Musician
Rachel Ray	Cook, TV Personality, Best-Selling Author
Michael Caine	Oscar-Winning Actor
Bill Cosby	Grammy-Winning Actor, Comedian
Jay-Z	Grammy-Winning Artist, Entrepreneur

Literary Legends

No College Degree to Start Career

Misfit's Name	Professional Claim to Fame
Carl Bernstein	Pulitzer Prize-Winning American Journalist
William Blake	Romantic Age English Poet and Painter
Ray Bradbury	American Writer
Charles Dickens	English Novelist, Social Campaigner
William Faulkner	Nobel Prize-Winning American Author, Poet.
F. Scott Fitzgerald	American Writer
Edgar Allen Poe	American Writer, Poet, Literary Critic
Tennessee Williams	Award Winning-American Playwright

Sports Icons

No College Degree to Start Career

Misfit's Name	Professional Claim to Fame
Pelé	3-Time World Cup Champion, Soccer
Wayne Gretzky	4-Time Stanley Cup Champion, Hockey
Kobe Bryant	5-Time NBA Champion, Basketball (as of 2010)
Roger Federer	15-Time Grand Slam Champion, Tennis (as of 2010)
Joe DiMaggio	4-Time World Champion, Baseball
Mario Andretti	4-Time Indy Winner, Auto Racing

And the Biggest Secret of All

I was never alone on my journey. Many mentors taught me the art of entrepreneurial thinking and the power of thank-you notes. From artists to executives, I'm grateful to all who shared their wisdom. Did anyone have the *true secret*? Hardly. Everyone has gaps and no one masters everything.

As for peak performers worth emulating, they share common threads. They listen and learn. They work and play with passion. They're willing to fail and try again. They're humble and appreciative. They embrace something that matters.

So our journey concludes as we began; proving a simple premise. With or without degrees, or gifts at birth, the secret to entrepreneurial thinking is connecting *4 Essentials* (skills, strategies, values, and purpose). As it turns out, these same success principles are the path to a real-world MBA — your **M**aster's in **B**asic **A**bilities.

Parting Wisdom

DARE TO DREAM

"It's kind of fun to do the impossible."
WALT DISNEY (1901 – 1966)
American Entrepreneur, Founder of Disney

WE ALL SCREW UP

"Experience is the name everyone gives to their mistakes."
OSCAR WILDE (1854 – 1900)
Irish Poet, Writer

LISTEN TO YOUR GUT

"Don't be trapped by dogma ... and other people's thinking;
Have the courage to follow your heart and intuition;
They somehow already know what you truly want to become."
STEVE JOBS (1955 – 2011)
American Entrepreneur, Co-Founder of Apple Computers

WISDOM COMES WITH TIME

"Life is a succession of lessons which must be lived to be understood."
RALPH WALDO EMERSON (1803 – 1882)
American Poet, Philosopher

ESSENTIAL PHILOSOPHY

"Maintain passion in your purpose and patience in your practice."
CLIFF MICHAELS (1967 – 1882)
American Writer, Strategist, Entrepreneur

Ready to Get Your
Successful Groove On?

CliffMichaels.com provides narrated e-courses and free tools for personal growth, career development, and entrepreneurial training. Visit today.

System 1: Personal Growth

Self-Discovery & Team Mission
12-Point Discovery

Communication & People Skills
Social and Business Intelligence

Problems & Conflict Resolution
The Art of Moving Forward

Teams, Forums & Boards
Brain Trusts and Effective Meetings

Focus & Time Management
Seize the Clock and Get Organized

Goal & Project Planning
Action · Accountability · Alignment

System 2: The Entrepreneur's Edge

Launching a Business
Idea to Execution

Power Negotiations
The Art of Leverage:
Price · Package · Preparation

Sales • Marketing • Branding
Driving Relationships and Revenue

Leadership & Motivation
Inspiration · Style · Strategies

Angels, Demons, & Venture Capital
Money · Mergers · Risks · Rewards

Finance + 8 Steps to 800 Credit
Wealth-Building Formulas

Sign Up for Cliff's Blog
Stay in touch on Facebook and Twitter

www.CliffMichaels.com

The Story Contest

Now it's your turn. I want to learn from you.

Who were your strongest influences and why?
What's your story (funny, inspirational, educational)?
Which of *The 4 Essentials* were most critical to your success?

The most popular submissions will earn cash,
free training courses, and a spot in my next blog or book.

RULES, FORMS, AND CONTEST ENTRY

CliffMichaels.com

Giving Back

With each book you purhase,
a FREE book is donated to a student.
10% proceeds also go to charities.

Group rates > email: specials@cliffmichaels.com

About The Author

Cliff Michaels is a writer, speaker, and social entrepreneur. Along his journey, he's been a strategist, angel investor, real estate broker, and high-tech CEO. Having trained thousands of clients in personal growth and entrepreneurship, Cliff's lessons are now available at CliffMichaels.com. His result-oriented courses and tools enable anyone to find their path to a **M**aster's in **B**asic **A**bilities.

Cutting his entrepreneurial teeth with street-wise mentors, Cliff bought his first home at 19 with no money in the bank. His unique experience as a college freshman inspired research to prove a simple theory — that a gap existed between classroom education and real-world *Essentials* critical to success. After dropping out of USC as a sophomore, Cliff spent the next 20 years building companies in real estate, technology, and consulting. His companies have closed over $500 million dollars in sales.

Today, Cliff's mission is to inspire, give back, and raise the bar for education, personal growth, and entrepreneurial thinking. He lives in Santa Monica, California where hobbies include yoga, tennis, hiking, travel, and long catnaps.

Interested in Booking Cliff?

Speaking ~ Consulting ~ Training ~ Live Retreats

www.cliffmichaels.com